Ext for Dad Job
1123

you have to be the one to Start
the rumer in order to be Sued

MEDITATION

Inspiring | Educating | Creating | Entertaining

Brimming with creative inspiration, how-to projects, and useful information to enrich your everyday life, Quarto Knows is a favorite destination for those pursuing their interests and passions. Visit our site and dig deeper with our books into your area of interest: Quarto Creates, Quarto Cooks, Quarto Homes, Quarto Lives, Quarto Drives, Quarto Explores, Quarto Gifts, or Quarto Kids.

First published in 2018 by Wellfleet Press,
an imprint of The Quarto Group
142 West 36th Street, 4th Floor
New York, NY 10018 USA
T (212) 779-4972 **F** (212) 779-6058
www.QuartoKnows.com

Wellfleet Press titles are also available at discount for retail, wholesale, promotional, and bulk purchase. For details, contact the Special Sales Manager by email at specialsales@quarto.com or by mail at The Quarto Group, Attn: Special Sales Manager, 401 Second Avenue North, Suite 310, Minneapolis, MN 55401, USA.

10 9 8 7 6 5 4 3 2 1

ISBN: 978-1-63106-633-7

Cover and Interior Design: Ashley Prine, Tandem Books

Printed in China

This book provides general information on various widely known and widely accepted images that tend to evoke feelings of strength and confidence. However, it should not be relied upon as recommending or promoting any specific diagnosis or method of treatment for a particular condition, and it is not intended as a substitute for medical advice or for direct diagnosis and treatment of a medical condition by a qualified physician. Readers who have questions about a particular condition, possible treatments for that condition, or possible reactions from the condition or its treatment should consult a physician or other qualified healthcare professional.

IN FOCUS

MEDITATION

 Your Personal Guide

JACQUELINE TOWERS

WELLFLEET
PRESS

To Ian Cooper for his
understanding, patience, and
encouragement during my writing, and
to my spirit guides for their inspiration.

CONTENTS

1

ABOUT MEDITATION

We all live busy lives these days, so this is a way of removing ourselves from the rigors of daily life for a while and getting back to our true selves.

—Lynne Lauren

Erroneous Beliefs

Meditation is calming but it isn't hypnotic. When you meditate, you are awake and aware, although you need your surroundings to be peaceful and non-intrusive. Meditation is often relaxing, but that's not its main purpose. You do not need to concentrate hard or even focus on a specific matter, and while some of the meditations in this book do have a specific purpose, others just allow you to let go of the real world and get closer to your inner self. You don't need to empty your mind, although some meditations can help you to push unwelcome thoughts out of your orbit. Neither do you need to meditate for hours on end. Ten minutes might be enough on some occasions, but you can progress to twenty or thirty minutes of meditation if you want to.

Although some religions advocate sitting in the lotus position, it is unnecessary, as it is far more important for you to be comfortable. You don't need to be religious or spiritual; or interested in angels, spiritual guides, gods and goddesses; or anything else of a metaphysical nature to meditate.

Meditations aren't something you need to work at because they just *are...* and anything that results from them will raise your level of awareness—even if your only initial awareness is that you are so tense that you find it hard to meditate. There is no race to the top, no prize to be won, and nothing to be gained or lost. Meditation is a helpful practice for any person, for any purpose, and for any season.

What Is Meditation, Anyway?

In some respects, one could call it a mental and physical form of aerobics, but without the physical movement or mental exertion. Confusing? No more so than "the sound of one hand clapping," which is a fascinating Zen paradox. A number of definitions exist, so it is easier to say what meditation may *achieve* than it is to define it—such as increased calmness, physical relaxation, improved psychological balance, better coping with illnesses, enhanced general well-being, and mutually improved links between body and mind.

Recent medical studies in the USA have intriguingly claimed that meditation can reduce blood pressure, and even reduce symptoms of irritable bowel syndrome. It can very likely help with symptoms of anxiety, depression, and insomnia, but it isn't regarded by the medical community as being capable of actually *curing* disease. Meditation is considered safe for healthy people. If you have any doubts, first ask a professional tutor and your own doctor as well. It pays to be safe rather than sorry where your health is concerned. Most certainly, don't ever replace conventional medication or care with meditation, and don't use it as an excuse to postpone seeing your doctor about a medical problem.

In Control

Many forms of meditation involve developing better control of your body and mind. For example, specific meditations frequently require defined methods of breathing during the meditation.

Where, When, and How to Meditate

While it would be nice to have a room that you set aside for meditation, this is unlikely to be practical, so a bedroom, a quiet sitting or dining room, a sunroom or conservatory, or your back garden are all fine, as long as you can be left in peace for a while. It's best if the room is decorated in gentle, pastel colors, because strong, bright colors can be intrusive and energizing.

You need somewhere to sit in comfort. Some people like to lie down, some sit cross-legged, and others prefer to sit, but whatever you choose to do, you need to be comfortable. Avoid tight clothes because these will bother you.

You might prefer to meditate in the morning in order to prepare for the busy day that lies ahead, but if you aren't a morning person, you might want to make some time for yourself in the evening, as long as you aren't too tired. In the worst case, you will doze off, which is probably not a bad thing. Just try again another day when you aren't as tired.

Some people find sitting and meditating difficult, especially if they try to do it on their own, so you might be better off working with a group with someone acting as the leader who reads the meditation to the group. This kind of activity is called a "led" or "guided" meditation, because someone has to lead or guide it.

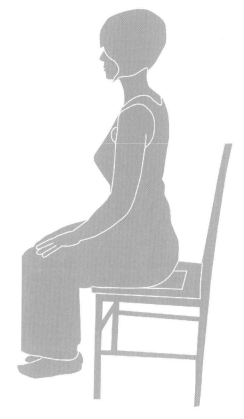

Opening, or Preparatory, Meditations

Opening meditations are quick and simple, but you may need more than those, so I have included some deeper preparatory meditations of various kinds. Some are important for grounding, while others enable you to open your chakras, which is important for those occasions when you want to do something spiritual or metaphysical.

Chakras are the seven psychic centers that line up along the body from the base of the spine to the crown of the head. You will discover more about these mysterious centers later in the book.

Mental and Physical Benefits

In addition to the spiritual factors, meditation provides mental and physical benefits, such as these:

- Reduces stress.
- Eases headaches.
- Reduces high blood pressure.
- Eases insomnia.
- Eases anxiety.
- Enhances self-esteem.

- Improves mood.
- Increases memory retention.
- Improves the immune system.
- Increases energy levels.
- Encourages creative thinking.
- Enhances creativity.

It has been scientifically proven that meditation creates changes in the brain and the way it responds to situations, so it helps us deal with daily stresses and problems that life can throw at us. It can help us deal with pain, with certain medical conditions, and with mental blocks, so that memory and creativity can be improved. Meditation may even boost the immune system. It helps balance the body's systems in all areas of physical and emotional well-being, and the more it is practiced, the greater the benefits.

Over the centuries, meditation has developed into different branches that address different problems and needs. Today's world vastly differs from medieval times, let alone a couple of thousand years ago. Some of the current forms used worldwide are discussed below.

MOM

Remember, meditation equals MOM (mind over matter). You may come across wildly optimistic claims as to the healing powers of meditation, often in conjunction with offers of training at substantial monetary costs. Use your common sense and never forget that there are limits to any healing process, and meditation cannot cure serious diseases. It is useful for certain purposes, usually in spiritual or mental needs. It can help in alleviating pain, or at least in controlling reaction to pain, shocks, and upsets, but it is not a panacea for all ills.

Various Meditation Techniques

Guided Visualization

This is a recent technique, yet it originates from Buddhist monks. In this concept, rather than letting the mind go free, you concentrate your mind on a specific matter or situation. This may be something that requires attention, or it may just be something on which you wish to gain further understanding and appreciation. You should focus on positive and relaxing thoughts, using these as guides to eliminate all other feelings from the mind. If guided visualization is used consistently, the benefits range from stress relief, through spiritual upliftment and healing, to many other enhancements of your personal skills and abilities.

Heart-Rhythm Meditation

This form of meditation concentrates your inner energies on developing your own conscious abilities. The heart will normally be the prime thought focus, but regular, deep breathing is emphasized throughout the session. You may expect to feel improvement in physical, spiritual, and even emotional directions. Stress handling and improved appreciation of life are additional benefits.

Kundalini

This is a deep form of meditation, and the intention is to activate the Kundalini energy lying dormant as a coiled serpent within the base chakra at the lower end of the spine. The meditation concentrates on arousing the serpent's energy and flowing it upward, through the other six main chakras and along the spine toward the crown chakra above the head. Healing is one of the benefits of this powerful meditation, but the main intention is to attain spiritual perfection and the ability to experience different states of consciousness.

Mindfulness

Here is another system that owes its origins to ancient Buddhist traditions. Its value in today's world is high, as it addresses and helps to alleviate many of our day-to-day worries, stresses, and uncertain, indecisive behaviors. The mind is allowed to wander and to drift into a relaxed and quiet state. Breathing slowly and consciously is the key to successful mindfulness meditation, although it should not interfere with the acceptance and understanding of passing thoughts and images. Regular use of mindfulness has been shown to reduce conditions of depression, anxiety, and similar mental conditions that abound in our stressful Western way of life.

Qi Gong

The origins of Qi Gong come from ancient China, and it is one of the oldest forms of meditation. It leans more toward physical improvements such as better respiration and posture than to mental and emotional ones. Invariably, these improvements lead to more confident, relaxed, and easier mental abilities. You combine breathing, physical movement, and mental techniques to drive energy forces through the chakra centers and around the body in general.

Transcendental Meditation

The Transcendental Meditation® movement, started by Maharishi Mahesh Yogi in the 1960s, has been one of the popular and very well known organizations of recent times. The technique uses a specific form of mantra meditation, most commonly performed while seated in the basic lotus position, which involves crossing the legs with the feet resting on top of the opposite thigh. This pose is common in Hatha Yoga, but it is difficult to adopt unless one's knees and leg tendons are very flexible. Practice makes perfect, as the old saying goes, but if one still finds it too uncomfortable, an option is to use the "half-lotus" position: this calls for only one leg to be placed atop the opposite thigh; the other leg can be left loose under the opposite thigh.

Zazen

One of the easier forms of meditation, Zazen comes from the Zen Buddhists in Japan. The name translates as "seated meditation" and the posture is self-evident. One typically sits on a flat mat called a *zabuton*. A cushion called a *zafu* is also used, while other variations include sitting on a chair. One should be relaxed but not so comfortable that one falls asleep.

The intention is to allow thoughts, ideas, and images to pass through one's mind without becoming involved or judgmental about anything that one experiences. Separating oneself from all experiences while being aware of them is a very powerful form of self-control and gaining inner spiritual development.

In Japan, Zazen is often performed together with a number of other practitioners in a meditation hall called the *zendo*. A ritual begins and ends the session, with the participants bowing to their seats and then to each other.

Mantra Meditation

A *mantra* is a short phrase that is repeated during a meditation cycle. Concentrating on the phrase helps to keep out other thoughts, and in time, one develops a spiritual understanding of the meaning of the phrase. Mantras may be spoken or chanted out aloud.

Om Namah Shivaya

Yoga and the Lotus Pose

Yoga is the type of physical activity most often used in conjunction with meditation. Meditating styles and yoga postures frequently include sitting, standing, and lying variants. Choose whatever suits you—many people have back pain problems, and lying down on a padded yoga mat is perfectly acceptable; just don't get so comfortable that you fall asleep!

Some of the yoga asanas, or positions, can be difficult for the elderly or disabled to achieve, let alone to maintain for some time. The best solution is

Ignore the Itch

Learn to ignore the little itches that plague you when you're quiet and unmoving. You've probably always scratched them subconsciously, but when meditating, they are a distraction. Believe it or not, you can ignore them! With some practice, you can master the urge to scratch, and then you can rejoice in being more in control of your body.

consult a professional yoga tutor, who will help you to work out a suitable plan.

The lotus position (Padmasana) features in many branches of meditation, religious and otherwise. It consists of crossing the legs with the feet placed on top of the opposite thigh. When this position is done correctly, the knees should be flat on the ground, and the feet close to the abdomen. Keep the spine straight and the head and neck muscles relaxed. A cushion may be needed in order to stay balanced and not fall back. An easier version of the lotus position is called Sukhasana or the Burmese pose. It is simply the way you normally sit cross-legged—feet on the ground, not on the thighs. However, there is a tendency to fall or lean forward, so a cushion under the knees may help.

The lotus position can be difficult to achieve. Even if you have trained your legs to obey your command, you may need a cushion to maintain your balance (zafu). To bring the body forward into a balanced posture, sit on the front of the cushion, with legs on the floor. The lotus position is suitable for lengthy meditation or contemplation.

Enclosed Meditation Cards

Included in this book are seven guided meditation cards you can use to relax, refocus, and re-center at any time and any place in your practice. One side contains a guided meditation, and the other side an illustration to serve as a visualization tool for the meditation.

2

HISTORY AND RELIGION

There is no path to happiness: happiness is the path.

—Buddha

Background to Meditation

Meditation goes back thousands of years and is practiced by most religions, albeit in different ways. It is sometimes called by other names and often takes different forms. If you are a newcomer to meditation, you should look into a range of beliefs and systems to find one that is closest to you and with which you feel most comfortable. This chapter can give you only a brief introduction into the vast range of meditation practices used in various religions. Furthermore, meditation is not limited to being part of any religious beliefs— it is a widely held system of self-improvement, spiritual enhancement, and healing processes.

It is thought that meditation originated from Hindu traditions of Vedantism around 1500 BCE, but archaeologists think it goes back at least five thousand years. The ideas spread to China via the Buddhists in the fifth and sixth centuries BCE and formed part of Taoism.

In the religious writings of Hinduism and Buddism, the word *dhyana* (meditation, contemplation) occurs, and it is evidently taken from earlier Jainist sources. Meditation is essential in Jainist beliefs; it differs from Buddhist and Hindu meditation in that its aim is to avoid negative karmic entrapment, rather than being a positive route to spiritual upliftment.

As far as can be established, the roots of meditation evolved within the Sramanic religious movements in distant, pre-Buddhist times. Austerity and renunciation were common practices in these movements, prevailing until recent times, when less drastic traditions evolved. The Hindu Vedas refer to a monk-like way of life as part of commitment to the strict, ascetic traditions of the time.

Chanting

Repetitious names and phrases are not uncommon in religious forms of meditation.

Close links exist between yoga and many meditation systems, and one of the earliest treatises on yoga—the Yoga Sutras of Patanjali—dates back to at least 100 BCE.

Much later, the famous Bhagavad Gita ("The Lord's Song" in Sanskrit), an extensive discourse involving yoga, meditation, and spirituality in poetic form, enlarged upon these matters. Meditation itself forms a vital part of the Gita's discussion of Bhakti Yoga. Exactly when the Gita was written is unclear; it could have been anywhere between about the fifth and second centuries BCE.

In the eighth century CE, Japanese interest in Buddhism began to grow and localize. A strong and extensive culture developed.

Religion and Meditation

Buddhism

The Buddhist texts are the source of many forms of meditation. In most cases, the goal is to further your progress on the path to nirvana and enlightenment. Common features are breathing exercises and concentration on past or present experiences and ideas. Different regions or countries have developed specific forms of meditation that suit

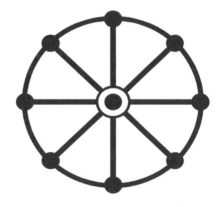

their way of life, so the Buddhist practices have become quite flexible, although still very similar in purpose. When Buddhists meditate, they usually take this to a higher level than most. Their meditations can be accompanied by chanting and the ringing of a bell.

Christianity

Christian religions often refer to
contemplation or contemplative prayer
instead of meditation. There is a
difference in emphasis as well. Whereas
Eastern meditation is generally accepted
as developing your own spiritual abilities
or helping to heal yourself, Christian
emphasis is more on the connection to
God and seeking his wisdom, guidance, or
help in dealing with life's problems as well

as reaching communication with, and becoming more attuned to, the omniscient
power of God. Forms of meditation have more in common with prayers than
the mantras of Eastern systems. Catholics meditate through prayer and
thinking of Christ, sometimes with the aid of rosary beads. Surprisingly, it was
as late as 2013 before the Catholic Church formally approved of meditation.

From at least as far back as the fourth century CE, a major form of
meditation has been the "Sacred Reading," or *Lectio Divina*. This form dwindled
over the centuries to being used only by monks in their monasteries, but it has
shown a strong resurgence in recent years. Nevertheless, it is too academic a
form for general use nowadays. Today, we are more interested in meditation
that is easier to understand and use on a daily basis without interfering with
our daily lives.

Hinduism

Many different schools of Hindu
meditation exist. Yoga is often used
in preparation for the beginning of
a meditation session, and there are
yoga postures, or asanas, that can be
maintained while practicing certain
meditations. The Hindu objective of
Moksha is similar in concept to Nirvana
in Buddhist teachings.

Today's religions practice meditation in various ways. For instance, Hindus look upon meditation as an inward journey, believing that when they are at peace within themselves, everything outside their bodies will be in harmony. Unlike Westerners, they do not sit rigidly trying to undo the things that are giving them stress, because to them, meditation is on a higher plane, and it includes doing no harm to others—be they insects, animals, humans—and ultimately becoming God-conscious and at peace with themselves. This, therefore, de-stresses their lives automatically.

Jainism

The aspirations of Jains when meditating are quite different from those of Hindu and Buddhist followers. The intention is to prevent karmic attachments and negative activity rather than to attain spiritual goals and self-improvement. Ascetic and austere practices used to be features of Jainist meditation, but the extreme practices have become less common and have been replaced by more-modern beliefs.

Sikhism

Attaining spiritual objectives and performing good deeds are inextricably linked with meditation practices in Sikhism. The intention here is to achieve closer contact with God, ultimately becoming one with the divine. Sikhist beliefs include the need for frequent meditation (simran) on, and recitation of, the divine name (Naam).

Taoism

Taoist practitioners have the usual links to Buddhist thought. However, they have turned their attention more to the inner self, represented by the personal solar and lunar energies within. These variations include specific methods of breath control, concentration, visualization, and mind empowerment with the aim of achieving high levels of Qi (physical) enhancement.

THE NEW AGE

◆

Westerners were introduced to meditation in the 1960s when the New Age reached the West. The Beatles got a lot of publicity for their visit to India, where they met a guru called the Maharishi Mahesh Yogi. He taught them meditation, which much influenced their music at this time. The Beatle who was most into Indian music and Indian practices was George Harrison, while Ringo Starr was the least interested and stayed in India only a couple of days.

Native Americans

Native American Indians visit a sweat lodge or smoke peace pipes and meditate, usually accompanied by drumming and chanting, while they connect with nature and their spirit animals.

Judaism

Most Jews these days don't tend to meditate in a formal manner, and those who do so tend to refer to it as "contemplative practice," which involves prayers, chanting, and breathing with the "intention" as to what they want to focus on.

Islam

Moslems believe meditation to be a very important aspect of their lives, as it enhances their spiritual development and can be a way of discovering solutions to problems.

※ ※ ※

3

EQUIPMENT AND PRODUCTS FOR MEDITATION

Technology is just a tool. In terms of getting the kids working together and motivating them, the teacher is the most important.

—Bill Gates

Meditation is the least expensive activity you can engage in because it doesn't require any equipment. You can meditate while sitting on the grass, perching on a fallen log, or even sitting on the back doorstep, or you can sit cross-legged on the floor or on a chair. The results will be just fine in all those cases. If you meditate while lying down, you might doze off, and most people agree that sitting is the best posture for this task.

However, you might enjoy treating yourself to special equipment, and there is much from which to choose. For instance, if you are doing a combination of yoga and meditation, you may want to wear special clothing and buy a yoga mat—or you could buy a special Zen meditation stool that is made of natural materials or an oak bench to sit on. You may want to buy meditation cushions, called *zafus*, that help you sit cross-legged without slumping. You can buy New Age clothing or white pajama-type outfits. All these items are available online.

Silence or Sounds

Some religious orders meditate in silence and others might use breathing techniques, mantras, drums, chanting, or flutes. Westerners accept that relaxing music can help produce a meditative state. Playing soft music helps to calm stressful thoughts, and, to turn things around, it is known that some modern composers meditate *before* writing their music. Music can also be extremely healing, and it is interesting that many yoga practitioners use music to put their clients into the right state of consciousness, or they create their own music by chanting. Transcendental Meditation involves repeating a word or phrase as a mantra; this causes a slight trance-like effect, which is said to relieve stress.

Meditative Music

Some people love to play special "meditation" music, which you can buy in New Age stores, in the background while they meditate. Others find it gets in the way and makes it hard for them to switch themselves off mentally. If you find music of any kind too intrusive, don't play it while meditating.

There is much available in the marketplace, so choose what suits you best. Some people prefer the lilt of panpipes or soft music, while others prefer to listen to the sounds of nature such as rain, birdsong, or the calling of dolphins and whales. Native American chanting or drumming is also popular, as are recordings of Buddhist bells or singing bowls. It is a matter of finding what suits you and what you find the most relaxing. There are beautiful singing bowls available online and energy chimes with mallets for prayers, yoga, and meditation. The only things you *don't* want to listen to are loud music or tunes that demand your consciousness and are therefore distracting.

A quick and easy way to find music is on YouTube. There is so much to choose from, including Native American drumming, music, and chanting; African chanting; religious chanting; and Buddhist chanting, with one "Om Mani Padme Hum" chant being especially delightful. These pieces are long enough for many of the meditations in this book, but you may prefer to play them before you meditate to put you into the right frame of mind. You could run one of them in the background while someone is leading a group meditation.

Incenses and Diffusers

Most of us know the emotions that are stirred up when something unpleasant happens to us, so you can use any of the following to help with the feeling of well-being. It is known that "hugging a tree" makes you feel better and helps to ground you, so any incense stick or essence that you burn which is tree-based is of benefit to meditation.

Incense

Incense has been used for centuries, with frankincense, myrrh, and sandalwood being the most popular when used in conjunction with meditation. Nowadays, there are numerous incense stick aromas to choose from, and it is down to individual choice as to which will benefit you the most, depending on the reason for your meditation.

Sprays

There are many products in the marketplace, so it is possible to purchase room sprays and/or body sprays in various aromas. These days, you also have a variety of aromatic air fresheners. Choose whatever suits you and the situation on which you are meditating.

Candles

It is possible now to buy scented candles in practically all aromas. These can also be used while meditating, and will not only create the perfect ambience but also aid your well-being.

Essential oils

These can be obtained in many combinations. An inexpensive way of achieving similar results as a room spray or scented candle is to pour some essential oil onto cotton balls and then place them into an open jar.

Warning! All of the above may be used while meditating, but make sure you are not allergic to the scent or substance. Also, be extremely careful when using incense sticks, candles, or anything with a naked flame. Always make sure you place your items on a safe surface and consider all safety aspects.

Wood- or Mineral-Based Essence or Incense

CEDARWOOD

Cedarwood will give you the courage to carry on with determination and confidence.

SANDALWOOD

Sandalwood calms the mind and will give you inner peace. It encourages you to persevere.

CYPRESS

Cypress will help you to stay strong and it will help you cope with any transitions that may be taking place in your life.

MYRRH

Myrrh brings inner peace when emotions are overflowing. It helps to calm you and give you tranquility.

FRANKINCENSE

Frankincense is particularly good when meditating as it will slow down your breathing, and it will calm and center you.

Fruit Incense or Essence

Anything fruit-based is also surprisingly good with which to meditate.

LEMON

Lemon is known as a good cleaner and refresher, so it makes sense that lemon will also cleanse your thoughts and will lift your spirits. It will also give you clarity.

GRAPEFRUIT

Grapefruit can relieve any anger, frustration, or blame that you may be feeling. It will make you feel more optimistic.

BERGAMOT

Bergamot is perhaps not so well known but it is a great antidepressant and relieves anxiety. It will restore any lost energies, thereby giving you a more positive outlook. It will also make you feel more joyous.

Plant-Based Essences and Incense

LAVENDER

Lavender, which can be used in its raw state, is a marvelously soothing calmer and is great as an antidepressant. It encourages healing and forgiveness. It can also help you to relax so that you get a good night's sleep.

ROSE

Rose is perhaps the best essence to use to combat grief, as it guards against any shock you may have experienced. It aids against despair and loss, releases trauma, and encourages self-love.

CHAMOMILE

Chamomile is probably better known for its tea as a sedative to help with sleep, but it is connected to your heart chakra, and will ease overthinking and bring you back into balance. It is calming and helps to bring peace.

GERANIUM

Geranium will help you calm down so that you can communicate better during a stressful time. Inspiration will replace any hostility or anger you may be feeling. Geranium restores balance, thereby making you feel more secure.

GINGER

Ginger is known for its warmth, and this is particularly useful when your energies are low. Ginger releases the energies from your subconscious in order for you to achieve your goals. Therefore, it aids willpower and motivation.

4

MASTER KEY
MEDITATIONS

It does not matter how slowly you go as long
as you do not stop.

—Confucius

You need to use the Master Key meditation for preparation and grounding before doing any serious meditations, as this will link you to both the universe and the earth beneath you. Some meditations in this chapter are designed to help you relax and get into the zone, while others are for protection.

If you need to open your chakras before performing a particularly deep kind of meditation or before doing any kind of psychic work, you will find out how to do this in the chapter that follows this one. You may find that your chakras open quite easily without any specific help, but you will need to use the system outlined in the next chapter to close them again after meditation, if you want to avoid feeling spaced out or having bad dreams or other invasive experiences.

Everyone who wants to develop his or her psychic ability needs to meditate, as this will prepare the way by opening the chakras. The base chakra is the source of psychic and spiritual ability, and when the chakras that line up from the base to the crown are fully open, work such as clairvoyance, healing, Reiki, and so on is easier to carry out. It is true that the chakras will open of their own accord when one starts to work on a spiritual level, but it is much better to go through an opening meditation first.

Everybody I know uses meditation to relax, ease stress, and get into the zone for any kind of psychic work. My friends and I sometimes use meditation for practical purposes, such as dealing with obsessions or worries by getting the mind to detach itself from the person or situation that is causing the problem.

I have gathered the meditations in this book from several friends who work in the spiritual field. All of them are keen to share their knowledge and experiences with you, the reader of this book, and for you to learn how to use these techniques in a trouble-free manner.

A Master Key Meditation for Preparation and Grounding

This is a preparation meditation that will connect you to heaven and earth, and it puts you into the right state to make the best of any deep meditation that you wish to use.

- Focus on your breathing and imagine putting all your problems in a basket at your feet, and with each out-breath you become more and more relaxed . . . more and more relaxed.

- Now focus on your out-breath and imagine roots coming out of your feet and pushing down deep into the earth. With every out-breath, they reach down deeper and deeper, and you become more relaxed. As you push your roots down, they reach deep into the core of Mother Earth. Then, focusing on your in-breath, begin to breathe those loving earth energies in and upward through your roots.

- The energy may be any color that you wish, but is often experienced as a ball of pure silver light, and as you gently breathe this energy up and up and into your feet, feel your feet become warmer and more and more relaxed.

- Breathe the energy up into your legs, and feel the warm and relaxing energy moving up through your calves, your thighs, and up toward your base chakra. See, sense, and feel your base chakra opening. Some people see their chakras as flowers with petals opening, while others see them as spinning vortexes or crystals of various colors— however you see, sense, or feel your chakras will be right for you.

- Continue to breathe the energy up through your body through each of your chakras until you reach your crown chakra. As the energy rises, you should see, sense, and feel it moving upward as a big, white, silvery light that continues traveling upward into the universe.

- See, sense, and feel the energy going up, up, and up to the very center of our galaxy and out into the center of the universe, as it seeks out and joins with the very core of universal creative energy.

- As you focus on your in-breath, turn the light energy from silver to gold and start to breathe this pure energy back across the universe and then bring it back down into your crown chakra.

- Breathe the pure energy down through your body and into your heart, filling your heart with unconditional love while you breathe this energy down through your body, letting it flow out through the soles of your feet and down into Mother Earth.

Now that you are connected in a loving way to the heavens and the earth, you can continue with any other meditation of your choice.

A MEDITATION FOR YOGA BREATHING

There are no hard-and-fast rules to meditating, so you will soon find what works best for you. For instance, I meditate in an upright position with my hands resting on my knees and turned upward. However, it is important you feel comfortable, and it is a good idea to wear loose-fitting clothes rather than restrictive ones. If you find it relaxing to have some soft music playing in the background, that is fine, but you need to be in a quiet place with no distractions, so make sure your phone is switched off and family members are unlikely to burst in on you.

Now that you are seated comfortably, concentrate on your breathing because you need to slow it down. A tried-and-tested method is to use the yoga breathing technique of breathing in for two counts, holding it for four counts, and exhaling slowly for eight counts. If you are already experienced in this method, then you can expand on the timings so that each inhalation and exhalation takes a little longer. Do your yoga breathing three times. Your next task is to take yourself through the protection and grounding process, which follows.

A Short Master Key Grounding Meditation

This kind of meditation links you to the earth and prevents you from becoming light-headed or "spacey." It also helps you achieve your aims when doing further meditations or if you do some channeling or healing work afterwards.

- Feel your feet on the ground and imagine your feet having roots.

- Imagine those roots going deep into the ground, pushing down deep into the ground, taking any negativity with them.

- With each out-breath, push those roots deep into the ground, deeper and deeper into the ground, down to the earth's rich molten core.

- Now focus on the base of your spine.

- With each out-breath, imagine the base of your spine getting longer and longer, pushing down deep into the earth, deep down among the rocks, pushing down and wrapping round something very solid so that you are truly connected to Mother Earth.

- Now you feel very safe and grounded.

- Imagine all negativity—any negative thoughts, feelings, worries—flowing down through your legs, down through your roots, down your elongated spine, and down into the heart of Mother Earth, where they are all transformed into pure positive energy by her unconditional love.

A Simple Form of Protection

- Sit or lie comfortably, close your eyes, and relax.

- See yourself inside a golden egg-shaped shell, but leave a small hole in the top.

- Allow golden light from the heavens to enter the top of the shape through the hole and fill the inside of it, surrounding you with the light.

- Close the top of the shape and focus on making the outside casing as strong as possible with the shiny exterior able to deflect any harm that may be directed toward you.

- Come slowly back to normality, open your eyes, and feel protected.

Protection and Clearing

- While sitting comfortably, be aware of your body and relax. If playing some soft music helps you to relax, this is fine.

- Now imagine you have a closed chimney in the top of your head, but there is a flap on one side of the chimney. You can choose either side of the chimney for this.

- Now draw down pure white light into the chimney through the flap.

- Bring the light down the one side of your body, starting with your head, shoulder, and arm, and continue to push it down your body, down your leg, and into your toes.

- The more light you bring in to one side of your body, the more you push out through the other side of your body the stress, worries, and negativity that fill your mind.

- Now imagine a second flap on the other side of the chimney, and keep pushing the white light in until you see black smoke coming out of the other flap.

- Keep bringing in the pure white light until it has completely replaced the black smoke. When the white light has filled your entire body, and only white light is coming out of the chimney, close the flap.

- You are now fully protected and ready to meditate.

A Simple Relaxing or Opening Meditation

This quick and easy meditation will put you into the right zone. You can play some gentle meditation music or just be quiet, and you can sit and do this one indoors or outside, depending on the weather and your mood.

- Sit comfortably and close your eyes.

- Imagine a small river and see a small boat tied up at the side of it.

- Untie the boat and climb in.

- Float down the river, enjoying the peace and the surrounding countryside.

- Keep on floating until you feel relaxed, and then climb out.

- Sit on the riverbank, enjoying the warmth and the slight breeze.

- Rest there for a while.

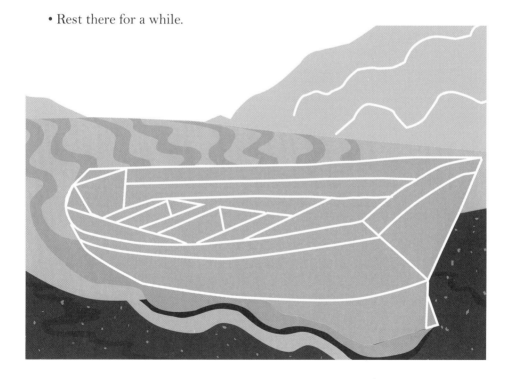

A Relaxation Technique

Close your eyes, relax, make yourself comfortable, and start to focus on your breathing. Breathe gently in and out, in and out, and say to yourself, "I am breathing in peace and love and breathing out all negativity. I am breathing in peace and love and breathing out everything I don't need in my mind right now." Do this until you become relaxed. Feel the gentle rise and fall of your chest as you gently breathe in peace and love and breathe out all worries and cares.

- Focus on each area of your body, starting with your face so that you feel the muscles around your eyes, your nose, and your mouth relaxing and releasing all tension.

- Focus on your neck and allow it to relax, and feel your head get heavy.

- Notice your shoulders and just let them drop, feeling more and more relaxed.

- You may feel your hands and fingers getting heavier and heavier or lighter and lighter.

- Feel the big muscles in your back release and relax.

- Feel your ribs breathing a big sigh, one by one, as you let the diaphragm go and relax down into your stomach.

- Feel the tension release from your lower back and your backside; let go and relax.

- Sense the tension leaving your thighs and your calves as the relaxation spreads down to your feet and your toes.

5

CHAKRAS

Peace comes from within. Seek it not from without.

—Buddha

About Chakras

Chakras are spiritual openings that run through the body from the front to the back, and each has a specific way of operating on a mental, physical, and spiritual basis. The seven main chakras line up along the spine as follows:

- The crown chakra is on the top of the head.
- The brow chakra (also known as the third eye) is on the brow, between the eyes.
- The throat chakra is in the throat and neck.
- The heart chakra is in the center of the chest.
- The solar plexus chakra is just above the navel.
- The sacral chakra is in the middle of the abdomen.
- The base chakra is at the bottom of the spine.

Each chakra is given a color that links with the rainbow, although there are some differences of opinion. This is the system that I use:

Chakra Colors	
	Crown: Purple
	Brow: Indigo
	Throat: Light blue or turquoise
	Heart: Green
	Solar plexus: Yellow
	Sacral: Orange
	Base: Red

Opening the Chakras

There are many methods of opening and closing chakras, but the following method is one from my friend Barbara Ellen, who used to be a consultant for the British Astrological and Psychic Society (BAPS) It uses well-known flower images.

- Gather light from the universe and bring the light down to your crown chakra.

- See the crown chakra as a purple lotus (water lily), and imagine it opening and allowing the light to enter through it.

- Let the light come down as far as the brow chakra, at which point a large blue eye opens up.

- Allow the light to come down as far as the throat, at which point a pale blue cornflower opens up.

- Let the light come down to the heart chakra, where some green leaves open up.

- Allow the light to come down to the solar plexus chakra, and see a large yellow daisy or dahlia open up.

- See the light moving down to the sacral chakra, where a large orange marigold opens up.

- Now let the light travel down to the base chakra, where a big red poppy opens up.

- Then allow the light to filter down through the legs and to fill the whole body and the surrounding aura.

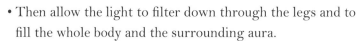

- Finish by imagining the light extending down into the earth, which means that you are now linked to heaven and earth by this light, with all your chakras opened and ready to work.

Closing the Chakras

It is actually more important to close the chakras than to open them, because they open of their own volition as soon as you do any kind of psychic or spiritual work. Chakras that have been left open can lead to bad dreams, feelings of psychic invasion, and other uncomfortable sensations.

- Start by imagining the light that has reached down into the earth being turned off, and turn off the light in your legs until you reach the base chakra.

- Turn off the light up to the base chakra and carefully close the red poppy.

- Next, turn off the light up to the sacral chakra and close the marigold.

- Take the light up to the solar plexus chakra and close the yellow daisy, while turning the light off.

- Now move up to the heart chakra, turning off the light as you go and closing the leaves.

- Move to the throat chakra, where you close the blue cornflower and turn the light off.

- Now bring the light up to the third eye, and close it firmly, shutting off the brow chakra.

- Push the light out from the crown chakra, and close the purple lotus flower.

- Finally, send the light off into the universe, where it can give healing to those who need it.

Chakra Clearing and Balancing

The following preparation and meditations for chakra clearing come from Joylina Goodings. These will help you clear blockages from your chakras and help to rebalance them. If you are tense, you can start with relaxation meditation to get you into the right state of mind. You will also need a brief grounding meditation (see the previous chapter).

Bottom to Top

Interestingly, some people prefer to open their chakras from the bottom upward and close them from the top down. Use whichever method feels comfortable to you.

Psychic Protection Meditation

The following meditation will protect you from unwanted psychic experiences, and it will help prevent the spacey feeling that can come after meditating.

See energy coming out of your crown, filling your aura and forming a hard transparent shell all around you. Notice the color of the shell, bearing in mind that any color or shape that you see is right for you. Only the energy of unconditional love can pass through this shell, and anything of a lower vibration will be transformed into unconditional love and sent back to wherever it came from. This shell is so impenetrable that only the highest good can pass through, so it protects you from both deliberate and accidental negative energies that affect you or your life.

Opening the Chakras

Some people see their chakras as flower buds opening, some as crystals taking on color, and some as spinning vortexes. However you see your chakras is the right way for you.

- As you breathe in, feel the energy come up into the base chakra and feel that chakra open, turning a brilliant shade of red. Feel that energy spreading around your base, filling your bones, warming and relaxing you.

- Now breathe the energy up into the sacral chakra, just below the navel. Feel the chakra turning a beautiful, brilliant shade of orange,

and feel the orange spreading all the way
around, round your hips, round the lower
tummy, relaxing
and warming.

• Breathe the energy up into the solar
plexus, feel the solar plexus open and
start to turn a brilliant shade of yellow.
Notice it feeling warm and happy. Feel
the energy spreading around your
midriff and back, taking you to new
levels of relaxation.

• As you draw that energy up into the
heart chakra, feel the heart chakra open and turn green, feel your
heart open, feel the unconditional love in your heart pouring out into
your aura and into the world. Feel the energy relaxing and warming
through your chest, both front and back.

• Breathe in the energy up to the throat. Feel the throat chakra open
and turn a brilliant shade of blue.

• As you begin to draw the energy up into your face toward the third
eye, feel all the muscles in your face relax, those little muscles round
the mouth, nose, and eyes relaxing. Your jaw relaxes as you draw
the energy to the third eye and you feel the third eye open and turn
indigo.

• In addition, as you draw the energy up to the crown, feel the energy,
and you may feel the crown of your head begin to tingle. Feel energy
coming out of the top of your head and tumbling down around you,
and cleansing your aura.

• Bring the golden energy down through your crown, down through
your body to your heart, and draw down the pure unconditional
loving energy from the gods. The energy passes straight through you
and down through your feet to replenish the energy of the earth.

Chakra Balancing

Imagine yourself stepping out of your body and noticing your chakras. Let go of judgment, just notice what you become aware of.

- How are the chakras spinning? Is one brighter, larger, or faster than the others? Is one more sluggish than the others?

- Do some appear more open than others?

- Are they all spinning in the same direction or in different directions?

- There is no right or wrong way, so just observe.

- Now imagine the earth and universal energies coming together in each of the chakras and bringing them into balance.

- Sense or see any blockages or dark spots being cleansed and released.

- Let the light that you see running through them make them all the same size, allowing them to fall back into balance.

- Give yourself as much time as you need to allow this to happen.

- Finally, step back into your body and feel all your chakras balanced and functioning normally.

Clearing the Chakras

This idea comes from Eve Bingham: Imagine crystal clear water entering your crown chakra and running through your body and out through your fingertips and toes. When you have finished, close your chakras carefully.

Closing Your Chakras

It is extremely important to close your chakras after any meditative or psychic work, as this prevents you from unwanted psychic vibes.

- Start to focus on the white light coming down through your body and filling you with healing energy. Feel the light push the colors down through your third eye, and see the third eye close and the indigo light fade away.

- As the white light continues down, you see and feel the throat chakra close as the blue fades away, and the heart chakra close as the green and pink fade away. You see and feel the solar plexus close and the yellow fade away; the sacrum closes and the orange fades away; and as the base closes, the red fades away. Now you see yourself as a pillar of white light connecting the universe to Mother Earth.

- Breathe, while you focus on pulling the roots from the earth back into your feet, and see or sense your chakras in your feet closing. Breathe and imagine your elongated spine retracting out of the earth and back into the base of your spine.

- Lastly imagine the chakra at the top of your head closing and cutting the cord of silver white light above your head, and let the universal energy drift away as your crown chakra closes.

- Begin to become aware of your body and your surroundings. Feel your body, wriggle your fingers and toes, and gently come back into the present and open your eyes.

You should drink a glass of spring water now, to clear your body and bring you back into the present. I also suggest that you keep a journal and write or draw your experiences for future reference.

6

MEDITATIONS FOR KNOWLEDGE

We think, we become.

—Buddha

If you are teaching or guiding others or running what mediums call "a circle," which is a group of people who are training to become mediums, or if you want to put on any kind of training session or workshop, these "knowledge" meditations are great openers.

The first meditation comes from Eve Bingham, a colleague who served as secretary for the British Astrological and Psychic Society (BAPS) for many years. This technique is what Eve calls an "intunement," which she used at the start of any teaching session to help students leave their everyday lives outside the room and get ready for their lesson. Her classes were usually on psychic subjects, but they could equally have been on astrology, handwriting analysis, or a complementary therapy.

The Woodland Pool

Put your bags, notebooks, pens, etc., on the floor by your feet. Sit back into your chair with your legs uncrossed so that both feet are on the ground. Rest your hands palm downward on your legs or in your lap. Close your eyes, take some deep breaths, and relax.

- Imagine you are walking along a path that wanders through a wood. The weather is just right, and you are becoming more relaxed as you stroll along.

- Notice the trees, plants, and birds and any other animals that you might see there.

- Soon you come to a pool. The water is still and quiet.

• Step into the pool and let it close over your head. The water is clear and you have no trouble breathing in it.

• Look around and see the books, equipment, tools, and knowledge that you need for your forthcoming studies.

• Pick up the particular knowledge and other things that you need, and slowly walk out of the pool.

• You will soon be dry, warm, and happy.

- Now take your precious goodies back along the path until you come to the edge of the woods.

- Step out of the woods and slowly come back to the room and to normal life.

- Open your eyes and get ready to study.

A Cavern of Knowledge

This is one of my own knowledge meditations. Start by protecting and grounding yourself by using one of the introductory meditations. Then, when you are ready, start here:

- It is a beautiful, warm, sunny day with a clear blue sky and your feet are bare as you walk along a soft, sandy beach. The tide is out and you find yourself walking toward a rocky outcrop. You look down and see a starfish that has been stranded in one of the rock pools, and then you see a baby crab scuttling away to hide under a large stone.

- You decide to clamber over the rocks, taking in everything around you, but the noise of children on the beach that you heard earlier has now faded away.

- Suddenly, you notice a cave behind an outcrop of rocks and you decide to go into it. On entering, you adjust your eyes to the darkness and you notice there are a number of separate caverns. Enter the first cavern, which contains a beautiful deep, blue pool. You bend down and run your hand through the water. Although the water is chilly, you immediately feel as if all your problems are sliding into the water and you feel revitalized and refreshed.

- You leave this cavern and go to the second, which has an orange-colored glow due to marine creatures that adorn the walls. You then see there are many different types of seaweed on the floor.

- You feel at one with your surroundings.

- You walk toward the third cavern, which appears to be red in color due to the makeup of the rocks. You immediately feel as if all your passionate feelings have risen to the surface. This surprises you.

- Without lingering too long, you are eager to see what the other caverns contain. You move on to the fourth cavern and find another pool, but this time it is green. You feel peaceful and happy when you place your hand into the water. It is not as cold as the water in the blue pool. You run your fingers through the water and have an overwhelming feeling of love.

- Excited now to see what the remaining caverns contain, you walk quickly to the fifth cavern, which is filled with beautiful purple amethysts that create a wonderful purple light. Feeling the spirituality of this cavern, you linger a little longer than you did in the others.

- You move on to the penultimate cavern, where you are greeted with a surprise. The cavern is made up of pure white crystal, which gives the impression that the cavern is fully lit. It's truly beautiful. Here, you feel at peace and at one with the universe. You are reluctant to leave, but your curiosity compels you to see what the last cavern contains.

- Feeling completely relaxed by now and still pondering what you have seen and experienced, you enter the last cavern. This is the most surprising cavern of all and it is certainly not what you expect to see. It is the largest of all the caverns and seems to be bathed in a yellow light, although you do not know where the light is coming from. There are bookshelves all round the cavern, which is because you have entered the Cavern of Knowledge.

- You leave this cavern but you now have the choice of which cavern you want to return to and spend time in. Linger there and consider why you went back to that particular cavern.

• When you have absorbed what you feel, it is time to leave the caves and return to the outside world. On exiting, you make your way slowly back to the beach. You notice more sea creatures in the rock pools. You begin to hear the laughter of children on the beach. Colors seem brighter. You feel the warmth of the sun. You see dogs happily running around, which is something you had not noticed before. Everything feels lighter and brighter, and you feel totally at one with your life.

Library of Knowledge

This meditation will help you find answers to your questions.

• Imagine yourself in the lobby of a large house.

• See a staircase and start to climb it.

• At the top, walk along a balcony until you see a second staircase.

• Walk down the stairs.

• Now enter a passage with doors on both sides.

• Each door opens into a room that has a library within it, but the knowledge stored in each room is different.

• Allow your intuition to lead you to the room that you need.

• Go into the room and examine the books, artifacts, and ideas.

> You may be aware of answers coming to you there and then, but you may not find yourself discovering the answers until the days and weeks that follow. If, as time goes by, something prods your intuition, listen to your heart, because the information will be coming to you from the wise spirit who inhabits the Library of Knowledge.

• You see someone sitting on a sofa, which is facing another sofa. This person may be male or female, young or old.

• The person is kind and compassionate and has only your well-being at heart, so sit down opposite the person and greet them.

• Ask the person anything you wish.

• When you the conversation ends, slowly come back to normal life and open your eyes.

❄ ❄ ❄

7

SPIRITUAL GUIDE AND ANGELIC MEDITATIONS

Every morning we are born again. What we do
today matters most.

—Buddha

The following meditations are spiritual rather than material or psychological, and they help connect you to the divine energies. The Flower of Life meditation came from Joylina Goodings.

Flower of Life

The Flower of Life is considered sacred among many cultures, although nobody knows for sure how old the symbol really is. The symbol can be used as a metaphor for the connectedness of all life and spirit within the universe, because it is a template containing many lenses. Not only does it represent divine feminine energy, but it also represents a window into the unity of infinity. The Flower of Life pattern is at the heart of an ancient Jewish belief system known as the Kabala. The Kabala required deep levels of prayer and meditation that were thought to ultimately lead to knowledge and understanding of God.

Meditation

Allow yourself some uninterrupted time. Turn off your phone, settle yourself comfortably, and begin to focus on your breathing. Put all your everyday worries into a basket at your feet, and let go of your everyday concerns. As you breathe, feel more and more relaxed.

- Imagine you have roots growing out of your feet and they are getting longer and longer and going deeper and deeper into Mother Earth like the roots of a tree.

- Imagine you are extending your spine, which is now lengthening and going down into Mother Earth.

- Now draw up the love of Mother Earth and feel the energy coming up as beautiful silver light. Imagine the compassionate energy of the divine mother who loves you unconditionally. Receive that love and feel it rising up into your heart chakra, filling it with the love of the divine mother.

- Now focus your attention on the golden rays of the sun and feel the loving masculine energy coming down through your crown chakra. Bring the energy down through your brow, your eyes, your nose, and your mouth, relaxing and warming until it reaches your heart chakra. Allow it to fill your heart with the love of the divine masculine energy of protection and acceptance. Feel yourself loved, protected, and accepted.

- Sense these two balls of light begin to merge, forming overlapping spheres of light, and sense the energy of peace forming in your heart and spreading throughout your body.

- Stay in this space and feel this energy spreading throughout your body. Sense the spheres within your heart multiplying and expanding, forming a Flower of Life in your heart.

- Now you may send these spheres to people, places, issues, wherever or whatever comes to your mind, so just breathe out bubbles of love.

- When you are ready, gently come back into the room.

Meeting Your Spirit Guide

You can start with any of the preparation meditations, but in this case, it would be a good idea to open your chakras before you begin.

- Imagine yourself outdoors on a nice day.

- See a staircase in front of you.

- Climb the staircase, leaving the day-to-day world behind as you go.

- See a hedge in front of you, and look for a gap in the hedge.

- See an opening in the hedge and walk through.

- You are now in a lovely garden. Look around so that you see and smell the flower garden and hear birds in the trees.

- You can see someone in the distance, but the spirit person is obscured by bright light.

- He or she is walking toward you. See what the spirit is like.

- Is it a man or a woman?

- Is it young or old?

- What race is the spirit?

- What nationality—roughly?

• Is the spirit dressed in modern clothes or old-fashioned ones?

• Ask the spirit who he or she is and what it can help you to achieve.

• Ask what you can do for the spirit.

A STORY ABOUT MEETING A SPIRIT GUIDE

My friend Roberta Vernon told me this story, which shows what happened when she was just starting to get into psychic work.

"My late husband and I were on holiday in Greece and we decided to take a tourist trip to Delphi. We walked up the hill to the Temple of Apollo, most of which had fallen down many years ago, probably as the result of an earthquake. There were some large blocks of stone lying around in the area where the ancient Oracle of Delphi was said to give her psychic readings.

"My husband was a very law-abiding man, but he surprised me by holding up the rope that marked the area where tourists were not supposed to go, and he shoved me under it while hissing in my ear, 'Slip down between the stones and keep out of sight while you tune in.' It took me a while to get comfortable—and to recover from my astonishment. I did as I was told while he and the rest of the tour group walked on to see the ancient "Olympic" running track farther up the hill.

"Not having too much time to spare, I did some yoga breathing and waited to see what would transpire—if anything.

"I soon saw myself in the Temple as it must have been when it was in use about 2,500 years earlier. I became aware of a tall, dark-haired priest who was filling small bowls with some kind of liquid, and sorting out lumps of incense, probably for a service that would be performed later that day. I coughed gently to get his attention, and he turned and smiled at me. He didn't speak at all but I clearly heard his voice inside my head. He told me his name and I asked if he would become my guide; he said he would. He also said there would be other guides who would visit me and help me with specific needs over the years, but that he would be the main one. This remained the case for about the next three decades, but eventually he joined the angels and I was assigned another main guide."

Now you can ask questions about what goes on in the spiritual realm, or you can ask your guide to help you, or you can just chat and get to know the spirit. Also, make sure that you ask your spirit to be there for you again when you need to talk.

- When you have finished, thank your spirit and say goodbye.

- Leave the way you came, go back down the stairs.

- Close your chakras and then come back to the day-to-day world.

The Temple of Angels

This meditation is a particularly spiritual one that will appeal to those who love angels and the healing energy of the cosmos.

- Breathe the energy of Mother Earth up and out while you notice the little muscles around your jaw, mouth, nose, and eyes relaxing and letting go as the warm, relaxing, healing energy rises up to your third eye.

- Feel the energy rising up to your crown chakra and sense the rainbow colors of the chakras combine at the crown chakra. Feel your crown chakra opening and feel the rainbow colors combining as you release pure white light and send it up and out into the universe, like a brilliant column against the night sky.

- Follow the energy out into the cosmos across time and space back to the beginning of time and the temple of angels, and know you are connected to all that is.

- As you reach the temple of angels, you find yourself in a circular chamber. You notice a small circle in the middle and it may or may not contain a seat. As you float across to the center of the chamber, you become aware that you are in a sphere—a sphere at the very center of time and space.

- Become aware that you are surrounded by choirs of angels that are all around, even above and below.

- Specifically notice twelve mighty angels, each shimmering a different color. As you gaze at the angels of the colors of creation, begin to notice the angels beaming colors of light at you. Each is sending a beam of light like a funnel of light straight into your heart chakra.

- Notice the mightiest of angels above you sending a beam of pure golden light right through your crown and into your heart. In addition, as you sit or stand within the sphere of creation, you feel completely connected to everything that is.

- You are the Tree of Life, the Eden tree, and as you breathe in, you breathe the pure love of the angels of creation through your crown and your heart, and as you breathe out, you send the energy down through your feet and roots and into Mother Earth. Allow yourself to be a channel of pure love, replenishing the earth. Feel the energy flowing through you to the earth.

- Focus on the peace and the love with which you are being filled, and sense and feel this energy flowing to all the parts of the world that need it. Send it to the world leaders and peacekeepers, spreading this energy and bringing peace and unity to all.

- Now it is time to return to your place on this planet, so thank the angels of the colors of creation and allow yourself to sink gently through the floor of the sphere, sinking gently back down, along the beam of light, back across the cosmos, and back into your body.

- Allow yourself to bring up your roots and gently close your chakras, starting at the base and working to the crown. See the colors fading away as you close the throat, the third eye, and the crown chakras.

- Gently come back to the world, open your eyes, and relax. Take a drink of water and give yourself time before rushing back into day-to-day life.

Finding Your Guardian Angel

We start this meditation with a chakra-opening technique.

- Feel your feet relax, and as your feet relax and become warm, notice that warm, healing earth energy coming up through your feet.

- Feel it drawing up into your calves, and breathe the energy up through your knees into your thighs. Feel those thigh muscles relax and let go of all tension.

- Feel the energy coming up into the base chakra and feel that chakra open, while turning a brilliant shade of red; feel that energy spreading around your base, filling your bones, warming and relaxing.

- As you breathe the energy up into the sacral chakra, just below the navel, feel that chakra turning a beautiful shade of brilliant orange and feel that orange spread all the way around, round your hips, round the lower tummy, relaxing and warming.

- As you breathe the energy up into the solar plexus and feel the solar plexus chakra open and start to turn a brilliant shade of yellow, feel that energy spread around your midriff, round your back.

- As you draw that energy into the heart chakra, feel the heart chakra open, feel the unconditional love in your heart pouring out into your aura and into the world, and feel the energy relaxing and warming through your chest both front and back.

- Breathe the energy up to the throat, and feel the throat chakra open, turning a brilliant shade of blue.

- Draw the energy up into your face toward the third eye, and feel all the muscles in your face relax as you draw the energy to the third eye and feel it open, turning indigo.

- Now bring the energy to the crown chakra, feel the energy at the top of your head tingle, and know the energy is coming out of the top of your head.

- Now the energy is tumbling around you and cleansing your aura. Draw the silver and gold energy of the universe down through your crown and down through your body.

- Be more and more aware of your connectedness to everything as you bring the silvery gold light down through your crown chakra and connect to the cosmic web of gold that interlaces everything. Connect to universal knowledge and wisdom and to knowing that you are divine.

How to Meet Your Guardian Angel

This meditation will help you meet your guardian angel:

- You will begin to notice a form of energy or a kind of color coming toward you with arms outstretched. Your guardian angel comes toward you gently, smiling and holding out arms and wings of love for you. You will recognize this energy because it has been with you through many lifetimes.

- Feel the energy, feel those wings enfold you, and feel the unconditional love.

- Listen to what your angel has to say, as it will answer some of your questions.

- If you don't see anything, ask your guardian energy to create a vision for you in your imagination so that you can give the energy form and focus. Then rest in the energy and see what comes to you. Your angel may show you a symbol, a word, an article, or a touch.

- Realize that you can return to this place and meet your angel at any time simply by asking for this to happen.

- Gently come back into your space, into your body, and notice how peaceful and relaxed you are.

- Become aware of the protective shell of silvery gold surrounding you, and know that only positive energy can pass through this shell and that any negative energy is sent back to its source.

- Know that you have reached a new level in your vibrational journey and that you can feel the vibrations and energy of your angel at any time.

- Begin to bring yourself back into your body and return to awareness.

- Gently move your fingers and toes. When you are ready open your eyes.

Drink a class of water to hydrate yourself.

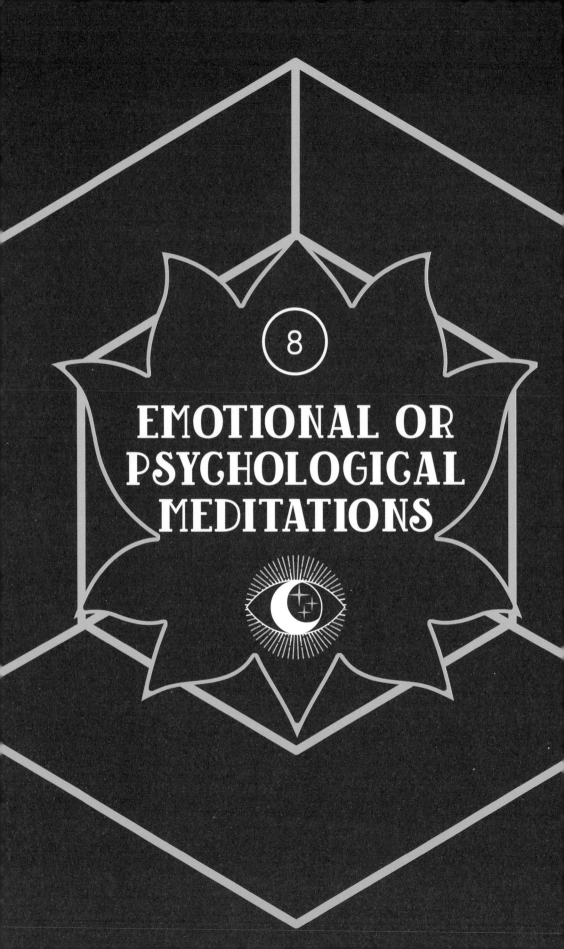

8

EMOTIONAL OR PSYCHOLOGICAL MEDITATIONS

Thousands of candles can be lit from a single candle, and the life of the candle will not be shortened. Happiness never decreases by being shared.

—Buddha

Stress Relief

This meditation uses the senses of sight, sound, smell, taste, and touch. It is designed to help you relax.

- Sit or lie with your legs and arms relaxed and your back straight.

- Begin to focus on your breathing, and notice the rise and fall of your lower abdomen as you gently breathe in and out, becoming more relaxed with each breath.

- Let go of any tension in your mind and body, and imagine putting all your problems, thoughts, and worries in a basket at your feet.

- Close your mind to the outside world while you focus on your breathing.

- In your mind's eye, find yourself on a beach. It might be somewhere you know or it can be an imaginary beach, but whatever it is will be just right for you.

- What kind of beach is it?

- Is it sandy or pebbly?

- What color is it?

- What color is the sea?

- Are there others on this beach or are you alone?

- Can you hear the sound of the surf?

- Are there any birds?

- Do you see children playing or dogs barking?

- What can you feel on this beach?

- Can you feel sand or pebbles beneath your feet?

- How do you feel inside?

- Are you excited or peaceful?

- How do you feel as you sit on this beach?

- What can you smell or taste?

- Can you smell the sea?

- Can you taste the salt on the breeze?

- What other scents and tastes can you sense on this beach? Perhaps ice cream or suntan oil. Perhaps hotdogs, flowers, seaweed, or anything else that brings back memories.

- When you are ready, wiggle your fingers and toes, gently open your eyes, and come back to this world.

Creating a Circle of Confidence

This technique is quick and simple. Once you have done it, you can create what is called an "anchor" so that you can summon up confidence whenever you need it. I find this one works best when standing up.

- Imagine a circle in front of you. It can be any color. Do not step into the circle; just see it in front of you.

- Now think about the matter that you need to feel confident, about.

- Go back to a time in your life when you did feel confident, when you succeeded and got a good result from something. If the event is similar to the one you have on your mind now, so much the better, but it doesn't need to be.

- Remember the event and allow yourself to experience those feelings of confidence in your body again. See yourself being confident in the future. See what you might be wearing, and whether you are standing or sitting. See a big, bright picture in your mind in which you feel supremely confident, and when you see this, you can step into the circle.

- Consider what you might need to make yourself feel even more confident. What are the qualities and skills you need? Is there anyone you like and admire who you can go to for help or who you can copy?

How do they stand? What do they do? See yourself the same way and bring all the qualities, skills, and so on into the circle with you, and notice how you begin to feel more confident.

- Come back to the present with more optimism about your future.

Fear of Change

Start with one of the preparation meditations, and follow with this meditation from Joylina Goodings that is designed to help you cope with change.

- Imagine what might happen in a perfect world, float out into the future, and see what your life might be in five years' time after you have made the changes.

- Ask your unconscious mind to tell you what kind of fear is holding you back, and ask your imagination to tell you not to worry and to know that the universal energies are shifting with your intention.

- Notice how you are feeling in your body. Sense this fear and, if it starts to feel overwhelming, just imagine how you might feel if you did not have this fear.

- Who would you be without this fear? How would you be? What would your life be like?

- When you have built up a wonderful picture of how your life would be without this fear, go back into your body and see where in your body this fear is holding you back.

- Ask your imagination to give it a form, a color, or a shape, and then have an imaginary conversation with it and give the fear a form that you now transform into positive energy.

- When you are ready, come back to reality and open your eyes.

Freeing Yourself from Past Hurts

The past influences every one of us, sometimes in good ways and sometimes in bad ways. A happy and well-supported childhood, youth, marriage, and career make for a great life, but most of us will suffer some form of injustice and unhappiness in our lives, and the memory of this can stay with us and affect our thinking and our decision making. Start by using a grounding meditation.

- Sit or lie down comfortably and close your eyes.

- Imagine a very long piece of ribbon with the ends sewn together so that it makes a circle.

- Now see the ribbon being twisted in the middle so that it forms a figure of eight.

- Visualize the person, problem, item, or situation that you want to remove in one "eye" of the figure of eight, while you see yourself sitting in the other "eye."

- See a large pair of scissors coming toward the middle point of the figure of eight.

- Now visualize the scissors cutting the figure of eight in half.

- Now notice the two halves of the figure of eight parting where the ribbons cross.

- Wish the other person, situation, or thing luck and say goodbye to it.

- Now notice the other half of the figure of eight floating away until it vanishes out of sight into infinite outer space.

- Come slowly back to awareness of your surroundings, knowing that the hold the problem had on you has now been cut away.

The pain should ease after this meditation, but if it is merely reduced rather than removed from your consciousness, do the meditation again a week or so later.

Another Method

This meditation is based on the same idea, but it is expressed in a different way from the previous one. It can help you detach from a person, place, or situation that has been getting you down for too long.

- Sit or lie down comfortably and quietly and close your eyes.

- Imagine a rope emerging from your navel and poking out in front of you.

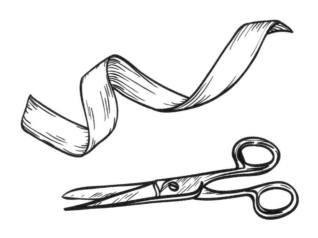

- See the rope growing ever longer.

- Notice the other end of the rope being attached to the person or situation that bothers you.

- Now imagine a pair of scissors cutting the rope at the other end so that the person, situation, or place detaches from the rope.

- Now imagine a pair of scissors cutting the rope at your end.

- See the person, place, or situation floating away from you and leaving you in peace.

- Slowly come back to yourself and open your eyes.

Trust that you will be able to put the past behind you and move into a better future. If you feel the angry and resentful feelings coming back to haunt you, do either of the previous two meditations again until you free yourself of the past trauma for good.

Quick Fix for Stress

This doesn't require peace, quiet, or even sitting down. Simply touch your thumbs to the tips of your index fingers while spreading out the other fingers. It is very similar to the "OK" gesture. Hold this position for a while and when you are ready let it go.

Opening Your Heart to Love

This meditation will release any blockage around the heart chakra, which may be preventing you from finding love, but it will also spread love around the world.

If you wish to use an essential oil to open your heart to love, use rose, rosewood, ylang ylang, or lotus. If you wish to hold a crystal, the right one is rose quartz.

- Draw in the divine feminine energy that you can see as a color—any color that you like—and bring the energy into your heart. Now breathe it out to the center of the universe and to the heart of creation.

- Draw in the divine masculine energy that you can see as a color—any color you like—and bring this down into your heart. Continue to take the light downward and into the center of the earth.

- Now you have created two columns of light that touch the center of Mother Earth and the center of creation, meeting at your own heart.

- Focus on the gap between the two columns of light in your heart chakra, and see or feel whether there is anything preventing these two energies from joining together in your heart chakra. If you feel a blockage, ask for it to be cleared.

- Ask what the blockage is and what is needed to clear it. Then imagine the two energies of unconditional love linking together in your heart.

- Send the love out through both the front and back of your heart chakra so that it reaches around the world.

Meditating for Love

If you think finding love or finding your soul mate is evading you, then it is normally your own fears that are preventing it. Your lack of love suggests that a deep-rooted blockage is preventing you from success. You need to meditate to discover what this blockage is and then to remove it. Listen very carefully to the first thoughts that come into your mind, and throw away the fear that is stopping you from finding the happiness and love you seek. Are you too afraid of letting go of your current lifestyle and enjoying doing what you want when you want? Have you subconsciously built a barrier around yourself? You need to get rid of these blockages. Put any dark thoughts and memories into an imaginary bag, tie it off, and send it out into the ether!

It is vital that you first accept yourself for who you are and embrace all your flaws. In other words, love yourself and stop being self-critical. How can you expect someone else to love you if you don't love yourself first? By doing this, you can then open the door for someone to walk through to you. It doesn't mean preening yourself in front of a mirror; it does mean telling yourself every day that you love yourself with all your faults. It won't be easy to let go of old habits or patterns, but by meditating and letting go of your old fears, you can change things for yourself.

Crystal Power

It might be worth holding a piece of clear crystal in your hand while doing these meditations, as this can enhance your desires.

Another factor that might hold you back is being too choosy. By that I don't mean asking yourself to settle for someone who is unpleasant, but you might be allowing yourself to go for only one particular type of person, while you ignore others. Try to be more open-minded, and give luck a chance.

Universal Law of Attraction

Meditating and visualization are great tools to put you on a path of change. While you are meditating, visualize who and what it is you want—but don't be too restrictive in your choices. Bring that love toward you. Ask the spirit world to send you your ideal soul mate, because your spiritual guides might have a better idea than you do about the most suitable partner—just be very clear when you are asking the universe to send you someone decent and worthy of your love. Your perfect partner is waiting for you, but you must attune yourself to receive him or her. Meditate and visualize yourself as already being in a relationship with Mr. or Miss Right. Feel the love you feel for each other.

While meditating, talk to your soul mate as if they are with you. Tell them *everything* about yourself—what your likes and dislikes are, what hobbies you enjoy, what music you like, where you like to travel, about your family, even problems you may be experiencing, and your faults as well—in other words, *everything*. If you do this, when your soul mate appears, they will already know everything about you.

Do this *every day*. It is all a question of reprogramming yourself to be able to accept love unconditionally. Instead of fearing love, more than likely subconsciously, you can look forward to it with excitement. Do not give in to doubts or give up. Giving up is a negative energy. You need to keep positive at all times and ask daily for what you want. You should not feel lonely or "left on the shelf," but savor the single life before it changes. Excitement awaits!

Meditating Against Loss

We have all been through loss, whether through bereavement or even betrayal. The loss one feels is indescribable, and the heart appears to feel the physical pain of loss. We've all heard the expression "my heart is breaking," and it is true that you go through a form of grieving. Can you ever get over it? Yes, of course you can.

Before embarking on this particular meditation, it is important that you sit quietly and ensure that you will not be disturbed. If you find lighting candles to be comforting, then light them, but make sure they are safe and not likely to fall over or burn the surface on which you place them.

Protect and ground yourself.

It is necessary to meditate specifically on your heart chakra so that you can let go of the feelings you are experiencing. You may find yourself crying while you do this, which is fine, as it is just a release of negative energies and emotions. If you do not let go of the emotions, you are in danger of becoming physically ill or angry, hurt, or afraid.

Do not be afraid to face your pain. Remember what has caused it, no matter how hard this may be. If you are able to achieve this aspect of the meditation, then you are on your way to taking back control of those feelings that have spiraled away from you. Release the emotion by crying, laughing, singing, or even dancing. If you are angry, then shout at the person as though they are with you. All or any of these are good for you as it will be your natural way of releasing your negative emotions.

If your emotions relate to a breakup, it is important that you are able to learn to forgive the person concerned. Hard as it may seem, it is essential for

EVERYTHING HAPPENS FOR A REASON

I am a firm believer that everything happens for a reason, even if we cannot see it at the time. When I went through my divorce after many years of what I thought was an ideal marriage, leaving me with two children to bring up on my own, I felt as if my whole world had collapsed. However, years later and on reflection, I realize it had released me to follow a new path that I would not have had the opportunity to follow if I had remained married. So, by accepting and embracing the new situation I found myself in, I was able to adopt a positive attitude. In my meditations, I kept saying "it's your loss, not mine," and this worked for me. That way, I was able to keep control of the situation in which I found myself and to deal with my emotions. I concentrated on moving forward and not letting the past hold me back. I achieved this through meditation and visualization of where I wanted to be.

your own well-being. What is the point of harboring the anger you may be feeling? It is only damaging you.

If what you are experiencing is through bereavement, visualize your heart and fill it with golden light. Use the "chimney" technique, as mentioned in chapter four, to push out the hurt and pain you are feeling. Continue to do this until your heart is completely filled with the golden light and there is no blackness left within your heart space.

Know that, despite the way you may be feeling, you are loved. The spirit world always sends love, as does the universe as a whole. You are never alone. Meditate and connect with the spirit world and with your higher self. Ask for the pain to be taken away in order that you can move forward.

These particular meditations will not work overnight, and they will need to be practiced over many days, weeks, or even months. However, they are great meditations to rid yourself of hurt, pain, depression, feelings of hopelessness, stress, or sadness, and they will provide you with relief and release, thereby giving you the energy to move forward.

❋ ❋ ❋

9

MEDITATIONS FOR TROUBLED TIMES

You will not be punished for your anger, you will be
punished by your anger.

—Buddha

The ideas here are a combination of magic and meditation, and they come from my friend Roberta Vernon. Some of my friends are extremely mystical, and they can tell you everything there is to know about rays, dimensions, and angels, while others are so well versed in spiritual philosophy that they can explain the vibrations that exist in heaven. Roberta has always been very down to earth, and she would shrug her shoulders if asked about such things, but she knows that there are times when living one's life in the normal way doesn't work and that and there are times when wishing and hoping are not enough. So my very non-mystical friend occasionally borrows ideas from the world of Wicca to bring about what she calls a "shift in the rift," meaning a way of nudging the universal energies into a better shape and direction.

Roberta's Words

Some people meditate to relax and others use meditation to develop their psychic or mediumistic talents. Many meditate for religious reasons, whether counting the beads on a rosary or contemplating the big questions of life and death. However, sometimes we are in desperate need for our little earthly lives to change for the better, and when this happens, we need to create a shift in the rift, as I call it. Sometimes we need to change something within ourselves, or we need to take on the more difficult task of changing something that is outside our control. The simplest idea really is good old-fashioned prayer, and a simple prayer to give you the strength to cope with a particular situation can help. However, sometimes it takes a bit more than this, and a combination of meditation and white witchery is needed.

For this, you will need to cast a spell, and this means creating a magical area, which some might call an altar. The area can be as basic or as fancy as you like, because the effect will be the same either way. While you may be tempted to create this in a bedroom, the best place is actually the kitchen or even the utility room. Magical and spiritual energies just *love* electrical equipment—all those films about lights flickering on and off or messages coming through the television aren't complete fantasy—although they are obviously made more exciting than they are in reality. So, doing your magical work alongside the fridge, microwave, washing machine, and toaster is all to the good.

Also, while we all love colored and scented candles, if there is any chance that a child or pet will knock them over, working on a kitchen counter, a metal draining board, or even in the kitchen sink could be the best place for this task.

These are the objects you need for your magical area:

- A tray to hold your magical equipment. If the tray is old and grubby, line it with some cooking foil with the silver side up. Avoid using paper or a pretty tray-cloth as it could catch fire.

- Two very small dishes, even eggcups, will do.

- A candle. This shouldn't be the enormous kind that takes days to burn down, as ordinary candles or tea-lights are perfect. The color is important, but I'll show you which to use for what purpose in a moment.

- An incense stick in a holder.

- Colored paper for your message. The color is important, but I'll show you which to use for what purpose in a moment.

- If you are a Wiccan, you will probably add a pentacle, but non-witches may prefer to leave this out.

The idea is to bring forward the energies of fire, earth, air, water, and spirit, so prepare your magical area in this way:

The Element of Water

Take one of the small dishes and pour a little bottled spring water, mineral water, or even a little collected rainwater into it. Tap water is all right but it contains chemicals, so pure water is better.

The Element of Earth

The obvious "tool" here is a crystal, and there are plenty to choose from, but you might want to consider what you are trying to achieve. The list below will give you some ideas.

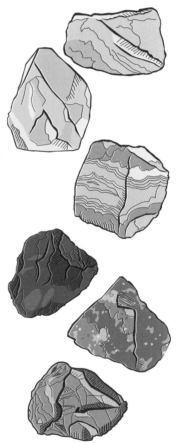

- If it is a matter of love, rose quartz is appropriate.

- Citrine, jade, or carnelian are useful for money and goods

- Health is aided by blue-lace agate or turquoise.

- If you need sex and passion, use a ruby or red jasper.

- Spirituality is enhanced by a dark blue stone, such as lapis lazuli or sodalite, and of course the purple of amethyst.

- If you need protection, use a dark stone such as obsidian or hematite.

- Finally, a clear crystal will stand in for any other stone.

Cleanse your crystal before you start by washing it in spring water (as long as it isn't a crumbly stone that will dissolve in water), dry it on some kitchen paper, and then hold it in your hands while visualizing white light coming down from the universe and energizing it.

If you feel the need for additional protection, find another small dish or eggcup and put a little salt into it. Salt is an ancient tool for protection from harmful influences, and it makes a link to the forces of the sea in addition to those of the earth.

The Element of Air

Your incense stick will give you the air element as soon as you light it. Incense sticks burn down quickly, so you might need another one for later, but if you just leave it alone, that is fine too. Choose one that smells right for you. For example, I dislike the normal "joss stick" smell, so I go for a lemony or cinnamon aroma.

The Element of Fire

A candle will give you the fire element. When selecting your candle, consider what you are trying to achieve. Also, bear in mind that, if you use two or more candles, while in theory they don't need to be the same color, you may be trying to achieve too many things at the same time. For instance, if you want to improve relations with your neighbors, find love, have a great holiday, get along better with your

father-in-law, pass your driving test, and get a great job, you would be better off doing several rituals over a period of weeks rather than all at once.

While there is plenty of information about color on the Internet and in books on spell-craft and candle magic, here is a quick reference in the meantime:

- Red for passion.
- Pink for love.

- Green for abundance.
- Light blue for good health.

- Orange for good relations with colleagues, neighbors, or friends.

- Brown or purple for success in business.

- Gold for success—for instance, in exams or testing circumstances.

- Blue or yellow to get the car fixed.

- Yellow or orange for fun.

- Purple for spiritual development.

- Black for protection (avoid black magic at all costs, though).

- White for any purpose.

Spirit

While not an element, spirit will definitely be present as soon as you start spell-casting. Always ask for the best outcome from your spell, even if it is intended to soften the attitude of someone who is bullying you. Never curse anyone and never set out to hurt anyone. Never try to make someone fall in love with you when you know perfectly well that they don't want you. Just work on making the universal energies better and on making yourself better. If you need money or a better income, ask for it but keep your requests reasonable— ask for what you *need*, not for the millions that you might fancy. In short, "for need rather than for greed."

The Message

A piece of colored paper is perfect for your message, and if you are a natural poet, you can write a rhyming spell, but if not, just write down exactly what you want, when you want it to happen, and how you want it to happen—in short, anything that will tell the universe exactly what you need. Choose the color of your paper to link with what you are asking for. If you only have white paper, that's fine, but you might find a colored pen that you can write with, as that would also work. The colors that I suggested for the candles are repeated below for your paper or pen.

	Red for passion.
	Pink for love.
	Green for abundance.
	Light blue for good health.
	Orange for good relations with colleagues, neighbors, or friends.
	Brown or **purple** for success in business.
	Gold for success—for instance, in exams or testing circumstances.
	Blue or **yellow** to get the car fixed.
	Yellow or **orange** for fun.
	Purple for spiritual development.
	White for any purpose.
	Black paper can be used, but you'll need a pen that contains silver, gold, white, or some kind of fluorescent ink so that your message will show up.

Light the candle and the incense and read out or recite your message three times, ending with words such as "so mote it be," "so be it," or "please, God" according to your personal beliefs and preference.

Put the message on the tray and let everything burn down. Now find somewhere comfortable to sit and perform a suitable meditation.

THE PINK SACK

At this point, you can use any meditation that suits your purposes, but this one works for those times when you feel overwhelmed by troubles. Record the meditation and play it back to yourself, or use it to lead others who want to meditate in a group.

This one is almost a take on the old World War I song that went "Pack up your troubles in your old kit bag."

- Sit comfortably with your eyes closed, relax, and listen to the recording.

- Imagine yourself standing in a nice space out of doors on a warm and pleasant day. Near where you are standing, you will see a pink cloth sack.

- Look at one of your problems and consider it from all angles, then pick it up and put it into the sack; tuck it well down into the sack, saying "goodbye, trouble."

- Pick another trouble and do the same thing, and then another until the sack is full, then tie it up.

- Keep doing this until everything that worries you, bothers you, irritates you, frightens you, or gets you down is tied up in a sack.

- Now take the sack by airplane, spaceship, on the back of a bird—or even on the back of a friendly dragon—and fly out into the universe. Fly beyond our galaxy and way past everything and everywhere, until you reach a planet where bad things are changed into good things.

- Now push the sack out of the vehicle and ask the beings on the planet to change the troubles from bad to good.

- Don't take the troubles back with you, because even when they have been softened or changed for the better, they are clearly too much for you to cope with, so leave them where they are for the hardworking creatures on the planet to work on.

- Open your eyes and know that you will soon feel better about everything.

❄ ❄ ❄

10

SPIRIT AND TOTEM ANIMALS

*Believe in yourself! Have faith in your abilities! Without
a humble but reasonable confidence in your own powers
you cannot be successful or happy.*

—Norman Vincent Peale

The following meditations will help you connect with your spirit animal.
You can find out the meaning of your spirit animal through many sources,
such as books and the Internet, and while many are based on Native American
Indian beliefs, not all are, so choose the system that suits you. Spirit animals
can be anything from a wolf to a dragonfly, but you should always be aware of
what comes to you first.

Music and drumming make sense with this kind of meditation, and there
is plenty to choose from on YouTube. While researching this book, I tried out
some Native American and African drumming, music, and chanting, some of
which is specifically designed for meditating, and it is all useful, if only to put
you in the right mood before you start your meditation.

Spirit Animal Meditation

Start with any of the protection or grounding meditations, or use a chakra-
opening meditation if you prefer. When you are ready, sit comfortably, close
your eyes, and begin.

- You are going to take a walk into the forest. It is a warm, sunny day
  and while you are walking along the path toward the forest, you
  become aware of what is around you. There are birds flying between
  the branches of the trees, and ants are going about their business at
  the side of the pathway.

- As you walk into the forest, you are aware the sunlight has become more dappled because the trees are casting beautiful patterns onto the forest floor. You continue into the forest until you find a clearing.

- It is a perfect patch of green grass with the warm sun shining upon it. Settle down and make yourself comfortable. Now you must just sit quietly and wait, but all the while make yourself aware of everything around you. Drink in the warmth of the sun and be aware of the softness of the grass where you are sitting. Heighten your awareness.

- You become conscious of a rustling sound, and you look in the direction of the noise and see an animal peeking out from behind a tree and looking at you. The animal walks cautiously toward you. It joins you where you are seated and sits with you.

- Wait to see if another animal comes to you. There will normally be only one or two.

- Now stand up and take your spirit animals back with you out of the forest. These spirit animals will remain with you. They are also known as totem animals or power animals.

Spirit Animals and Their Meanings

Each and every spirit animal has its own meaning. You will find that when you connect to your spirit animal, it brings to you what you may need or should be aware of. It is impossible to list every animal here, but I will list a few of the more popular ones. If your animal is not here, there is plenty of information you can obtain from books or the Internet. Spirit animals come in any form— mammals, birds, insects, fish, and so on. They can be the smallest to the largest and may even seem to be bizarre, but they all carry an important message for you and will stay with you throughout your spiritual journeys.

Ant

Ants are known to be hard workers and work as a team. They are incredibly strong for their size and communicate well with each other. These are the attributes the ant will bring to you. This tells you that, in order to achieve your goals, you should concentrate on the attributes you have within you.

Bear

This is a very powerful animal guide. Bears denote loyalty and strength, and they have a natural ability to lead through empathy and generosity. However, they tend to be somewhat introverted and can be dreamers. This animal shows that you should slow down and reflect upon what you really want and who you are.

Butterfly

This creature changes its shape, so it represents transformation. Unlike most spirit animals, the butterfly may have a message for you *now* rather than being a lifelong totem. So it may be urging you to make necessary changes to your life.

Cat

Cats are incredibly independent and can be somewhat mysterious. It is common knowledge that they are reputed to have nine lives. There is something magical about a cat (think of witches and black cats). A cat as your spirit animal tells you that it is worth taking risks through your own intelligence.

Deer

A deer brings you psychic awareness, healing, and gentleness as well as strength and renewal. It warns you against trying to force yourself on others but, rather, to look at things or situations in a new way. If you use love to change situations, then great adventures lie ahead.

Dog

Whatever happens in life, you shouldn't feel completely alone or abandoned, because your spirit animal will always be with you and it will always be a loyal companion to you.

Eagle

An eagle flies high in the sky independently and has incredible eyesight. Eagles also have extremely strong legs. Native American Indians believe the feathers of an eagle have great healing powers. Eagles bring you spiritual awareness, balance, and freedom. They will give you the insight you may need, and perhaps the ability to look at things from a different perspective.

Frog

A frog goes through transitions from the mere egg to tadpole and finally frog. Frogs represent new life and adaptability, as well as fertility and having enough money to live well. A frog is connected with water, which is associated with emotions. If a frog has come to you, then it is time to reassess

your emotions and assess what your aims really are. Maybe it is time to stop jumping from one thing to another—the frog will help you to adapt.

Goat

Goats can go where others cannot. This is a very strong spirit animal to have with you. You can call upon your goat when you feel you need balance within your life. With the goat, you can take up challenges that less confident people might avoid. The goat is also related to magical situations and will help you with your spiritual pathway. It will also help guard your reputation as well as enhance your sensuality.

Horse

Horses are strong, courageous, and
powerful animals. You can travel
long and far on a horse. Having
a horse as a spirit animal is an
indication that a change of direction
is worth considering. A horse will
provide you with the courage to
embark upon your new journey.

Jaguar

This is another very powerful spirit
animal. It is full of confidence, agility, and strength. In ancient times, the jaguar
was regarded as a shape-shifter. Jaguars are natural hunters, and if one has
come to you, you will be given vision and foresight as well as the confidence to
do what you set out to do. With careful planning, success can be achieved.

Lion

Known as the king of the jungle, the lion is considered regal. Lions are strong
and powerful with great courage. They are fearless but also very protective of
their family, so are quite peaceful until they feel threatened. The lion will give
you the strength and determination needed to stand your ground if and when
you feel challenged.

Monkey

Monkeys are known to be mischievous and
inquisitive creatures. Despite sometimes
causing havoc, they are very caring animals.
They are also quite creative and good at
problem solving. If you have a monkey as your
spirit animal, it is time for you to have some fun
and not to be stuck in a rut. Monkeys remind
you to keep a sense of humor about situations
in which you may find yourself. They also help
you to bring to fruition any new creative ideas
you may have.

Owl

One only has to think of Harry Potter
and Hedwig (the owl). Not only is the owl
connected with magic but with great wisdom
as well. Owls have incredible eyesight which,
in turn, will give you the insight and intuition
you need in certain situations. You will have
to become solitary in order to be receptive to
the message the owl wishes to impart to you.

Pig

This may first appear to be a strange spirit animal to have, but pigs are actually
highly intelligent animals and great problem solvers. The pig is also a symbol
of good luck, particularly in China, and are caring parents to their young.
Having a pig as your spirit animal not only provides you with these qualities,
but also will provide you with the intuition, wisdom, and luck you may need
when confronting certain situations.

Rabbit

Breeding like rabbits is a well-known saying, so it will come as no surprise that
rabbits represent fertility and abundance. They are also known to freeze in
fear in certain situations. The rabbit as a spirit animal will help you make quick
decisions when needed so that good opportunities do not pass you by. A rabbit
will also provide you with luck and abundance.

Rhino

This animal will stop you from stagnating and will allow you to make changes
whenever this is required. The rhino spirit animal also urges you to keep
secrets—maybe because some part of your life is confidential.

Spider

Not everyone's cup of tea, but if you think of the way the spider weaves its
intricate web, you cannot help but admire it. As you would expect, spiders are
industrious and work diligently. As spirit animals, they help you to maintain
balance within your life and to be creative. They remind you that everything
is connected, even within the spirit world, and that your actions could have a
great impact, so it is important to think things through carefully.

A WORD ABOUT BIRDS

Birds can represent freedom and travel, but in many traditions, they are messengers that warn of a death. The lovely robin is known as a particularly bad omen in just about every tradition that exists, while a sparrow warns that someone will die under strange circumstances. A friend of mine had her windows open on a hot day and a sparrow flew into the house, and it took her and her husband a while to get the frightened creature out again. Within days, one of her close friends died suddenly of a brain hemorrhage and then the same friend's wife followed him by dying unexpectedly in very odd circumstances.

Old lore says that crows will move out of an area if they sense that it is likely to be destroyed. In October 1987, a friend of mine noticed that a huge number of crows had moved into her suburban neighborhood, and she commented to her husband that the normal habitat of the crows would disappear within a few days. He was skeptical about this, but he knew that such old wives' tales sometimes have a basis in truth. Two days later, the great British hurricane struck southern England and thousands of trees fell down, including all the trees in the woodlands near my friend's home. It took a while for the crows to disperse and find new homes in areas where a few trees had survived the storm.

Tiger

Like lions, tigers are ferocious, determined, independent, and courageous. However, they are more focused and solitary than lions. As expected, these are the traits that the tiger will provide. They teach you to do things quietly, not to get distracted, and to be patient.

Wolf

The wolf is one of the most powerful spirit animals. It is an extremely intuitive pack animal that works within a team. Wolves are caring parents and good teachers to their young. A wolf as your spirit animal will provide you with the strength and knowledge you need, as well as protect you if you pursue your psychic abilities.

❈ ❈ ❈

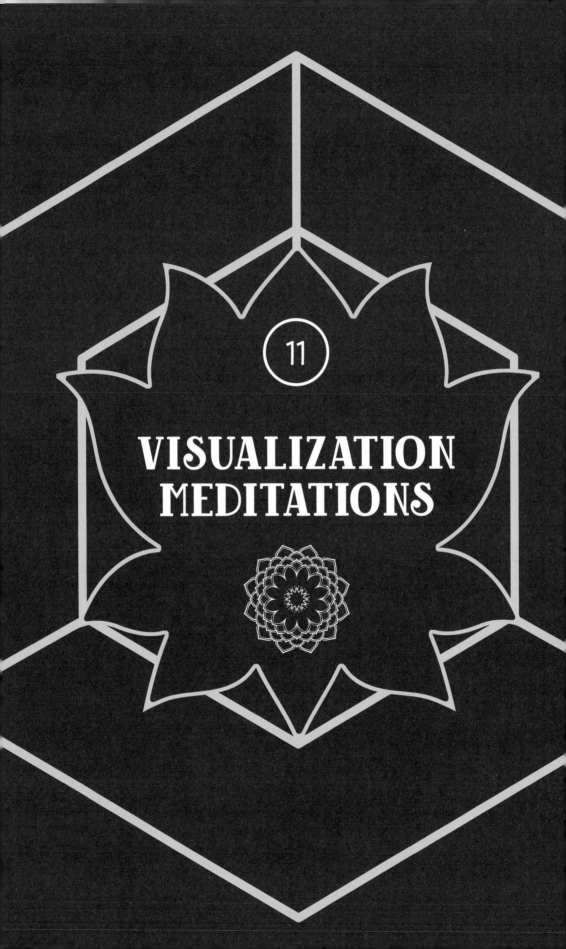

11

VISUALIZATION MEDITATIONS

Keep your eyes on the stars, and your feet on the ground.

—Theodore Roosevelt

The power of the mind is astonishing. You may know the saying "What the mind believes, it can achieve." This is never truer than when you are able to manifest what you want in life, as long as it is realistic. This can be done with meditation and visualization.

I know many people who do not necessarily meditate but create a visualization board. To do this, you need to write down all the things you want and concentrate on them on a daily basis. I actually did this when I moved to London with no job, just one friend, and no money. I wrote all these things down, repeated them as often as I could, and within a month I had a job, a new circle of friends, and money in my pocket. Once you are able to cross your immediate wants or needs off your list, move on to your new wants or needs. This method puts you in charge of your future.

Meditation will help you achieve visualization while you gain access to your inner self. Although very similar, meditation and visualization are not the same thing, but each can achieve effective results. For instance, many athletes have practiced visualization for many years. Meditation focuses your mind on your inner self, whereas visualization focuses on an image that is in your mind. It is advisable to learn how to meditate first, as you will find it easier to advance to visualization. Practicing both meditation and visualization can aid healing due to the hormones that the body releases while practicing. These techniques heal not only the physical body but also the mental state.

A Better Life through Meditation

It is possible to transform your life through meditation and visualization. For example, I know someone who used to be very shy, not very social, and who lacked confidence and was a very quiet person, despite being extremely clever and talented. A job interview was forthcoming about which the person was very nervous and anxious. It was recommended that the individual meditate on and visualize on what they really wanted. I am happy to report that the person is now vice president of a worldwide company, giving lectures and talks around the world to thousands of people!

A Black and White Visualization

There is a difference between meditation and visualization, but the following visualization bridges the gap. This is another exercise from Barbara Ellen, and she recommends it for those times when you are anxious, such as before a dental appointment, an important social occasion, a job interview, and so on.

- Sit down in a quiet place and close your eyes.

- Visualize a blank white wall in front of you.

- Now imagine a black spot in the middle of the wall.

- Watch the spot and see it gradually getting bigger and bigger.

- Keep watching until the black has replaced all the white.

- Now see a white spot in the middle of the wall.

- See the spot gradually getting bigger, until the white has replaced all the black.

- Notice a black spot in the middle of the wall.

- See the spot gradually growing until the black has replaced all the white.

- Visualize a white spot in the middle of the wall.

- See the spot gradually getting larger, until the white has replaced all the black.

- Now see a pink spot in the middle of the wall.

- This time the spot grows into a lovely rose that sits in the middle of the wall.

- Come slowly back to reality and open your eyes.

Train the Brow Chakra

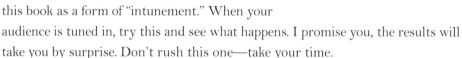

The brow chakra is also known as the third eye. This wonderful little party trick that is a great way to train people to visualize, and as you will soon see, it requires a little preparation. Gather your friends together and lead them through any of the opening or relaxing meditations in this book as a form of "intunement." When your audience is tuned in, try this and see what happens. I promise you, the results will take you by surprise. Don't rush this one—take your time.

- Ask your friends to sit quietly, facing you with their eyes open.

- Now hold up an object that has a distinct shape or color. It must be big enough for everyone to see it clearly, so it could be a book, cup, flower, vase, box of tissues, or just about anything you have on hand.

- Ask them to focus on the object for a while. It will become printed on their retinas.

- Now tell them to close their eyes and keep sitting still in the same position.

- Ask them if they can see the object in their mind's eye. Most, and perhaps all, of your friends will be able to do this.

- Now tell them to open their eyes. The object will still be there in the same position.

- Now ask them to close their eyes again.

- Ask if they can still see the object with their third eye.

- Ask if the object is as clear as it was before or even clearer. You might get a variety of answers to this question.

- Now, while they still have their eyes closed, very quietly put the object down, preferably where they can't see it.

- Pick up a second object—one that is a completely different color and shape.

- Ask your friends to keep their eyes closed but to tell you what they can see. Give them plenty of time to look, think, report, contradict each other, and add to the story.

- Ask them to open their eyes, see what you now have in your hand, and say whether this was the shape, color, or density of the item they were seeing with their third eye.

When you have recovered from your astonishment, ask a friend to select a couple of objects without you knowing what they are, and to take your place in front of the audience so that the others can have another go at training the third eye, while you have a chance to try the method yourself.

Seeing an Aura

This is another meditation from Eve Bingham, and it is designed to show you and your friends how to see an aura. A relaxing or opening meditation is a good start to this one, or you could use a chakra-opening meditation. After you have completed that, take the following steps:

- Stand against a plain background and ask your friends to gaze at your head and shoulders in a slightly unfocused way.

- Tell them to close their eyes. They should still see your outline on their retinas.

- Ask them to open their eyes again and look at you.

- Now ask them to close their eyes again, but this time to look outside the dark shape on their retinas and concentrate on the swirling colors that form around the dark shape.

- Now ask them to open their eyes.

Some may still be able to see a kind of shape or even a bit of color, even with their eyes open, but some will not. However, practice makes perfect, so they can try again any time they feel like it. Now ask one of your friends to take your place so that you can join the audience and have a go at seeing auras.

You can experiment by looking at your pets when they are resting, or even plants, as living things all tend to have some kind of aura around them.

PSYCHIC
TECHNIQUES

12

Your talent is God's gift to you. What you do with it is your gift back to God.

—Leo Buscaglia

Psychic development isn't a meditation technique in its own right, but it is linked with meditation and it is popular with those who are into spiritual work. Meditation not only enables you to connect with your spirit guides, angels, and spirit animals, but also aids with any emotional difficulties you may be experiencing. Besides all the beneficial aspects already mentioned throughout this book, meditation will enhance your psychic abilities.

Mediumship

Mediumship is connection with those who have passed over. A medium will give messages from the departed to their audience. Most mediums will meditate or "tune in" before giving a demonstration.

Should you wish to study to become a medium, I recommend joining a closed circle that most spiritual churches have, as it is essential that you are taught properly. Such circles can take place in private homes, halls, and so on. The essential thing is to ensure the person leading the circle is fully experienced and able to provide full protection to the students and to take control.

A circle is where you sit with a number of other people (usually no more than eight) with a circle leader. The leader is an experienced medium who will teach you how to communicate with higher sources and who will protect the trainees during the numerous different processes that will take place. Being able to hear from those who have passed over and receive messages from them is known as *clairaudience*.

Clairaudience

After protection and grounding, the students meditate and learn how to raise their vibrations, because the spirit world works on a much higher vibration than those of us on the earth plane. I always liken it to tuning in to a radio station. When you raise your vibration, you are attempting to reach the correct station. Sometimes this works very well and the messages are loud and clear, and sometimes it is difficult. The difficulty comes in not necessarily because you are doing anything wrong, but because those who have passed also experience difficulty in lowering their own vibration. What one hopes for is that the vibrations meet in the middle. This art of communication is practiced repeatedly when sitting in a circle.

When you become more experienced with mediumship, you may find that other abilities come to the fore.

MY FIRST MEDIUMSHIP

My first experience of attempting mediumship was attending a seminar. The medium who was giving the lecture asked for volunteers to give it a try, and I was extremely reluctant to get up as I went there only to listen to the lectures and knew nothing about mediumship. The lecturer pulled me off my chair and led me to the middle of the floor. She kept a hand on my back and asked me to pick out someone from the audience of fifty-six people. I was drawn to a lady who was sitting right at the back of the room. I closed my eyes and was surprised to find myself mentally looking at what appeared to be a television screen. I told the lady what I could see, and she came up to me after the lecture and told me that everything I had told her was completely accurate. It was this experience that encouraged me to join a closed circle, and in less than twelve months, I was doing platform mediumship work, which is where the medium stands in front of an audience and gives out messages from those who have passed over.

Clairsentience

Clairsentience is the ability to feel things from the spirit world. After meditating to connect with the spirit world, whenever I tune in to someone in the audience, the first thing I experience is what the spirit was feeling at the point of passing over. This is usually the medical condition they suffered. Obviously, this is sometimes unpleasant, but I just ask for it to be taken away, and the feeling disappears very quickly. Clairsentience also works on the clairvoyant level.

Clairvoyance

Clairvoyance means "clear seeing." It opens up the third eye, or brow chakra, which is in the middle of the forehead. Clairvoyants work on a lower level than mediums do. The information clairvoyants receive is more in the here and now, and it is possible to be able to inform an inquirer how his or her life has been, how it is at present, and how it will be in the future. Clairvoyants use their intuition and receive their information through either symbols or pictures. They are extremely sensitive to what is around them, so if you do this kind of work, it is important to know how to protect yourself against being bombarded with information.

When I was learning clairvoyance, I sometimes felt overwhelmed by the amount of information that was sweeping into my mind's eye. I could feel the emotions of both my living clients and from people who had passed on. I discovered that, along with help and advice from those who have experience in this field, meditation helped me to become calm and so I could control and limit the amount of information that wanted to come my way.

Other Psychic Techniques

A good circle leader will also be able to teach other methods to enhance psychic abilities, such as the ones that follow.

Psychometry

A psychic who is engaged in psychometry holds a piece of jewelry or something that belongs to another person and tunes in to see what he or she can pick up from it. It can be any item that belonged to someone who has passed over, or it can belong to a member of the group. The psychic will tune into the item given to them. It provides a link between the item and someone who is in the spirit world. The results are much the same as when working through mediumship. If, however, the item belongs to the person who hands the item over, the psychic will work more on a clairvoyant level.

Another form of psychometry is to take a photograph of a person and hold it in both hands while tuning in. To be honest, once you have mastered the way to tune in, you will find you can read anything. A couple of ideas follow.

Ribbon Reading

Psychics use different methods for ribbon reading, but it helps to know the meaning of the colors of the chakras. Here is my method:

- You'll need lots of different-colored ribbons. The lengths do not matter. Place the ribbons into a bag. It is not necessary to keep the ribbons straight; in fact, I prefer them to be all scrunched up.

- Ask the inquirer to take a ribbon out of the bag, preferably without looking. The color they have pulled out will be significant. For instance, red would tell me they are quite fiery, whereas if they pulled out a blue ribbon, they are good communicators.

- Take the ribbon from the person and feel it between your fingers. Be aware of every crease. Choose from which end you wish to start.

Now, whatever the length the ribbon may be, take it as representing a life of ninety years of age. If you halve the ribbon, it gives you the information of birth to forty-five years.

- If there appear to be many creases near the beginning, this indicates a difficult childhood or troubled teenage years. If there is a really deep crease, this indicates a trauma or big upheaval in the life of the inquirer.

- Keep working your way up the ribbon until you reach the end.

You will be surprised at the accuracy of the information you are able to impart. This is a great way to enhance your psychic abilities—and a good party piece or something that is quite fun to practice on your friends. I find that people love it.

Flower Reading

This is a variation on the ribbon-reading theme. You ask your friend (or client) to bring a small bouquet of flowers to you for the reading. The person must choose and buy the flowers herself, but they don't need to be expensive, as supermarket or gas-station bouquets are just fine. Once your friend is comfortable and ready for the reading, ask her to select a flower from the bouquet. Once again, the choice of flower us up to her. Your friend might want to make notes while you are doing your thing.

Starting from the bottom upward, read the flower as though you were reading your friend's life. If any leaves are damaged, it points to a difficult phase, but a smooth area of stem with a healthy leaf relates to a good phase. Go up the flower in this way and see what you can find. Ask your friend for feedback after the reading.

Crystal Ball Reading

The gypsy with the crystal ball is the standard image of the joke psychic, but while there are people who can read a crystal ball, they are very rare. This is how you train yourself to read a crystal ball—and believe me, you will need the patience of a saint.

- Buy a glass "crystal ball" rather than one made of actual crystal. Buy a new ball rather than using an old one or one that someone has given you.

- Soak the ball in salty water, or a solution of vinegar and water, for twelve hours.

- Wash the ball in running water, preferably in a stream or waterfall. Even standing outside and holding the ball while a heavy shower comes down would do the trick.

- Keep the ball in your pocket during the day and under your pillow at night. Do this for eight days.

- After eight days, sit with the ball in your hands and meditate upon it, by imagining white light coming down from the universe, filling and surrounding the ball.

- At the same time every day, sit with the ball and gaze into it, with your eyes going slightly out of focus.

- Eventually, you will see reddish clouds or smoke entering the ball from one side or another.

- Now you can invite a "client" to sit with you.

- Turn the light down low so that it doesn't glare, and sit your client down opposite you at a small table, with the ball on a stand between you.

- If there is still light around, a black cloth held against the ball will help.

- Sit quietly and wait for the red smoke, then as it clears, watch the images come.

- Any image that comes into the ball from the left will tell you about situations that are coming into the client's life.

- Any image that goes out of the ball to the right will tell you about situations that are moving out of the client's life.

- Tell your client what you see.

- Ask your client if he or she has any questions.

- See if the crystal ball will give answers to the questions.

Tarot Cards

Tarot cards were thought to originate during the fifteenth century, initially as playing cards, and they were not used for telling the future until sometime later.

There are numerous decks to choose from, and it is up to you to choose your own deck, but it is worth mentioning that there is a belief that the cards actually *choose you*. This certainly happened in my case.

A tarot deck consists of seventy-eight cards, each of which carries a picture symbol. There are twenty-two of what is known as the *Major Arcana* cards, and these are probably the most powerful in the deck. There are also fifty-six cards in the *Minor Arcana*, which, while less powerful than the Major Arcana cards, fill in the gaps and amplify the reading.

I always recommend that one find a good, reputable teacher when wanting to learn how to read the cards.

Like the ribbon reading, tarot is simply a tool that helps you pass on information to the inquirer. If I know beforehand to whom I am giving a reading, I always meditate on that person before they arrive for the reading, or before they telephone me for their reading, as this helps me to see if there is a particular message I need to impart. I love the tarot as the cards never fail me and each individual card really talks to me. I always say that I am just a messenger and that the words come *through* me, not *from* me. I know I have a spirit communicator who made himself known to me many years ago, and he goes by the name of Edward. I met him during a meditation, and he came to me—it was not a case of me looking for him. I consider myself lucky to have him and I have to say the information the cards impart never ceases to amaze me, even after nearly thirty years of reading them.

Open and Close

The chakras tend to open as soon as you engage in spiritual work, but if you have any problem with this, one of the chakra-opening meditations in chapter 5 will do the job for you. The most important thing is to close your chakras after heavy work of this kind.

I always leave mediumship to the end of a reading, so if I know there is someone waiting to communicate with the client, then I will bring him through. I find that the tarot combined with the mediumship helps give confidence to the client, so he or she feels that any messages that have been imparted should be followed.

I could go on forever about what it is possible to read with once you have mastered the art. I've given readings with sugar sticks over a cup of coffee. A friend of mine used to read beer mats when in the pub. The late David Bingham used to crush up a bag of potato chips (crisps if you are British), open the bag, and spill them onto a paper napkin and then read them! Another colleague is able to read African bones! Nothing is out of bounds once you learn how to meditate, protect and ground yourself, and give your higher thoughts the freedom they need. I have always said that anybody can do it—you just need to open your mind and meditation will help you to do that.

Remote Viewing

Where government-inspired remote viewing is concerned, the person or people who are being viewed obviously don't know this is happening and might not be happy if they did know. If you wish to try it, ask a friend to go somewhere—like the local shopping mall or a local beauty spot—and make an arrangement to "view" them at a certain time and try to "see" the friend and their surroundings. If the friend at the other end of the line opens himself to you by thinking of you at the same time as you are tuning in to him, it makes it easier.

Meditation and Auras

What is an aura? An *aura* is the electromagnetic egg-shaped field that surrounds your body and normally spreads out to an area of three feet. It is made up of seven layers and colors. These are known as the physical, astral, lower, higher, spiritual, intuitional and absolute layers.

Physical Layer Sleep helps to keep this layer healthy and repel negative thoughts and emotions. It is necessary to keep this level healthy and in balance.

Astral Layer When this level is out of balance, it harbors emotional thoughts, outbursts, and sensitivity. Doing something you enjoy and connecting with nature help to heal this level.

Lower Layer If you are experiencing a feeling of agitation, then this is the level that is affecting you. Doing too much work or thinking too hard will affect this level.

Higher Layer This level is all about self-love, so if you are being too hard on yourself, that will affect the balance of this level, and people around you will notice your change in behavior. It shows that you need to be kinder to yourself.

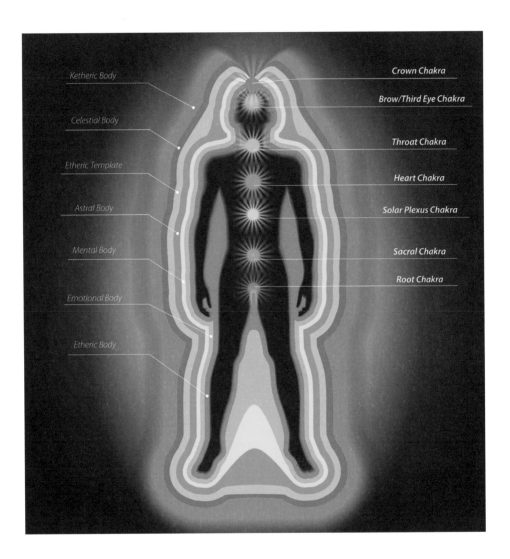

Ketheric Body

Celestial Body

Etheric Template

Astral Body

Mental Body

Emotional Body

Etheric Body

Crown Chakra

Brow/Third Eye Chakra

Throat Chakra

Heart Chakra

Solar Plexus Chakra

Sacral Chakra

Root Chakra

Spiritual Layer This level connects you to the universe. You will find that you will make connections with people who think the same as you and who will be able to teach you. When on this level, you may encounter antagonism from others, but you need to concentrate on like-minded souls.

Intuitional Layer Whenever you get a eureka moment, then you are on this level. You will find your creativity increases, and you will feel peaceful and calm. This is your spiritual level.

Absolute Layer This level acts as a balance to all the other layers. It is your destiny level.

Colors

When you learn how to see and read auras, you will normally see only one color surrounding the person. However, on rare occasions, you may see a rainbow of colors coming out of a person. This is a strong indication that the person is a very attuned healer. If you are projecting any color, this is what it is saying:

Chakra Color Connections	
	White This color indicates that you are very spiritual. It is also a color of protection.
	Silver This color shows that you are able to empathize with others. It also shows that you can be very intuitive.
	Red If this is a bright red, it shows that you are a passionate person who oozes confidence. If it is a dark red, it indicates that too much anger and frustration is being harbored.
	Orange This shows that you are an extremely creative person and is usually associated with writers, musicians, and other creative people. You are adventurous and full of energy.
	Yellow If this is a bright yellow, you fear that you may be losing control. If it is a light yellow, this indicates you are following your spiritual pathway, but that you still have a lot to learn. If the yellow appears slightly muddy in color, you have lost your way and feel that events or emotions have overtaken you.
	Gold People who emit a gold aura have reached their spiritual level and are calm and peaceful.
	Green This is a healing color and you may find you are able to heal or are someone who teaches or helps others. If the aura is a muddy-looking green, you need to take more responsibility for your actions and not pass the blame on to others.
	Blue This is the color of communication. If you emit a blue aura, you are a sensitive, empathic, and intuitive person who is a good communicator, both on the earth plane and with the spirit world.

Chakra Color Connections

	Violet This color shows that you are highly enlightened and spiritual.
	Brown This color relates to the earth, so you are probably someone who works out of doors with nature.
	Black Although it is rare to see black surrounding a person, it indicates that they are going through an extremely traumatic time emotionally.

When meditating to enable you to learn how to see auras, it is important that you sit quietly in front of a blank wall that is not covered in patterned wallpaper, posters, or pictures. Use yourself as your test. Either you can use your intuition through the meditation with your eyes closed or you can use your own hand. Concentrate on your hand to the point where you see a soft haze around it. You will then notice color appearing. This practice, whether physically or mentally, requires great concentration when you are starting out but becomes easier and quicker the more you practice it. As time passes, you will gain the ability to see auras clearly.

Meditating and Automatic Writing

If you have never tried automatic writing, then you should. By meditating, you can connect to your spirit guides or angels to provide you with answers to any questions you may have. It is a great way to channel information. First, you need to make yourself comfortable. I prefer to sit on my bed with my knees up so that I can rest a writing pad on them. However, some of you may prefer to sit up to a table. Do whatever suits you best. You will need paper and pen for this meditation.

• Protect and ground yourself.

• Wait until you feel you have made the connection with your spirit guides or angels. This can take some time, so do not try to rush to gain your answers. You have to allow time for your guides to absorb and process the information you have imparted to them. Close your eyes and concentrate on your questions.

MY EXPERIENCE WITH AUTOMATIC WRITING

This exercise can be amazing. The first time I practiced it, I didn't know what to expect. I thought I would give it a go after hearing about it, and because I enjoy writing. I was used to writing a daily journal, so I thought, why not? I remember writing down the problems I was facing at the time and asking for help as to what I should do. I wrote a lot until I felt I had poured out everything I wanted to get off my chest. I then stopped writing, put my pen down, made a connection with my angels, and pleaded with them to give me some advice. I didn't expect anything specific from them.

I waited for about fifteen minutes before picking up my pen again, feeling that I was compelled to write. Words just flowed from me so quickly that I didn't have time to process what I was writing. After about five minutes, I felt that I could read the written words. To my utter amazement, not only were there answers to my questions but also some excellent words of guidance and advice. I couldn't believe it! Everything made sense. It provided me with a sense of calm and reassurance, and I was able to move forward in a more sensible way.

My angels never let me down, but they do have fun sometimes, and as I mentioned, when practicing automatic writing, you may find your guides or angels showing you that they have a sense of humor!

- Start writing as if you are writing a journal. You must be specific in the question or questions you want to ask, and they must be genuine questions. Thoughts or words will come to you. Write everything down, even if sometimes it doesn't make sense. Do not think about what you are writing—just write.

- When you feel you have written all you need to for this particular session, stop writing and thank your spirit guides or angels.

- Wait a while before you read what you have written. You may find that you have to read it several times before the answers reveal themselves to you because the words may initially seem to be garbled.

❋ ❋ ❋

13

REINCARNATION MEDITATIONS

A people without the knowledge of their past history,
origin and culture is like a tree without roots.

—Marcus Garvey

Past Life Regression through Meditation

There are those who think past life regression can be achieved only through hypnosis but this is not the case. Past life regression can also be achieved through meditation. What a lot of us do not realize is that we subconsciously carry our memories from our past into our current lives. Have you ever wondered why certain situations keep cropping up over and again? Is it a repeating pattern? Have you ever felt a déjà vu moment? Has a place you have visited for the first time felt unusually familiar? By meditating to explore your past life, you can unlock the answers.

My first experience of past life regression through meditation was in a workshop attended by many people. One would think that this environment would be too distracting, but you go so deep into yourself that it is just you at one with yourself. Obviously, it is better to perform this meditation alone; I feel it is essential that you have the peace and quiet after the meditation, as it is extremely powerful and intense. This meditation requires the whole of your focus. Do not worry if it does not work for you the first time you try it, as it takes practice. You will find that your meditation will bring to the fore those things that may be holding you back. You will be unlocking subconscious memories from a past life. This particular meditation can help to speed up any healing processes you may need.

To do this meditation you must be totally relaxed, so make yourself comfortable in a chair, slow down your breathing, and protect and ground yourself, as you are about to connect to your very soul. Close your eyes, and starting from the top of your head, very slowly work your way down to your feet, relaxing every muscle and sinew in your body.

- Visualize youself standing by a river.

- On the bank where you are standing is a small wooden boat.

- Climb into the boat and push away from the shore into the middle of the river.

- It is only now that you realize there are no oars with which to row the boat, so leave yourself to the mercy of the river and see where it takes you.

- When the boat comes to a stop against the riverbank, climb out and walk along the pathway alongside the shore.

- When you reach your destination, take in what you are experiencing. Take note of the surroundings, any noises or smells, or the people you may encounter. Be observant.

- Ask why you have been brought to this place. What is it you need to know?

- Is there another pathway for you to follow? If so, do not be afraid to take it, as there will be another setting for you to explore and experience. Is there someone who meets you? If so, who is this person? What do they want to say to you?

If you find any of the experiences becoming uncomfortable or traumatic, remember that you are in control. Instead of "living" through the experience, just become an observer instead. When you feel you have had enough—and this is a meditation that can be repeated at any time, so there is no rush—make your journey back along the pathway to the boat you left on the shore, push it back into the river, and drift back to where you started.

Once back, bring yourself back into the here and now slowly. Be aware of your body again and bring the strength back into your limbs. Drink a glass of water.

Past life regression after carrying out a meditation can reveal some amazing things, for instance, why you might be afraid of spiders, or maybe you are afraid of being in an accident of some kind. Perhaps you feel comfortable in certain places or are easily annoyed by certain people. In other words, all sorts of things that may have been a mystery to you before could have a reason based on a past life event, and now you will discover what you need to know. Never be surprised at what comes through to you. Watch and listen carefully.

Reincarnation

There are those who believe in reincarnation, not so much in the West, but certainly in Eastern countries where they believe the soul must reincarnate in order to gain every experience possible. However, reincarnation is not endless, so once all the lessons have been experienced and learned from, the soul moves on to a higher level.

It has been said that some children can recall their previous life in minute detail, which turns out to be true. Dr. Jim Tucker wrote a book called *Life Before Life: A Scientific Investigation of Children's Memories of Previous Lives.* He interviewed 2,500 children whose memories were from things they had never previously experienced or who had birthmarks or scars identical to those they had in their previous lives.

If you have been described as "being wise beyond your years," then you probably had past lives that you can explore through meditation.

My Experience with Past Life Regression

My first experience was to find myself in a beautiful valley surrounded by luscious green hills with a crystal clear river running through the middle. I was in a Native American Indian encampment and I was the daughter of the chief. I was wearing exquisite gold and turquoise jewelry. It was a scene of peace and tranquility (something I was not experiencing in my own life at the time). I took this as a specific message to reassure me that all would be well and things would work out in the end.

I then took another path and found myself as a Roman centurion marching along with others. I was aware of everything I was wearing, down to the leather sandals. This told me that I would have to prepare myself for battle.

A friend of mine had a large birthmark running down his side, which always created curiosity, and he discovered, through past life regression meditation, that he was once a Native American Indian who had been speared in the side during a tribal war. Was this a past life memory or reincarnation?

※ ※ ※

14

MINDFULNESS MEDITATIONS

Work out your own salvation; do not depend upon others.

—Buddha

Meditation and Yoga

It is generally known that yogis have practiced meditation for many years, although the word used these days is "mindfulness" when relating to meditation. Nevertheless, while meditation is currently popular, it is also a very old technique, and yoga and meditation have been practiced together for centuries.

Yoga is not only about the physical benefits that one can achieve through the various exercises but also about meditation. Many large companies now use meditation and yoga techniques for their staff because it de-stresses and refocuses them so they find it easier to do their jobs. Yoga is also particularly beneficial to those workers who are desk-bound during their working day, and it has even been made available to over a thousand employees of Google; if that isn't a recommendation, I don't know what is! Not only does it improve the efficiency of those who partake in it, but it also has the benefits of lessening stress and anxiety and of preventing burnout for those who have to cope with a stressful environment. It can also boost the immune system.

Yoga, combined with meditation, is all about training the mind to focus, together with learning how to slow down the breathing. For those who may not be familiar with yoga, one usually sits on a mat and starts with a breathing exercise. Breathing is an important factor with yoga, as it is with meditation.

I suggest you start with taking in a breath for a count of two, hold

that breath for a count of four, and then slowly exhale for a count of eight. As you become more practiced, you can increase these numbers. This breathing exercise is perfect if you find yourself losing focus on what you should be doing and will help you concentrate. Whenever I find myself in a stressful situation, I use this breathing technique—and it is great for reducing high blood pressure. After the breathing exercise has been completed, your yoga teacher will instruct you to strike various poses, but without straining yourself in any way. This now becomes a slow form of exercise.

Yoga also uses chanting—usually "Om," which you hold for as long as you can. You will feel at complete peace while doing this, so you can leave it there, or use this as a preparation for whatever meditation you decide to perform. So now, place protection and grounding around yourself and take your chosen journey.

Mindfulness

Mindfulness is a mixture of meditation, psychology, learning to live in the present rather than chewing over the past or worrying about the future, and gaining a measure of perspective. Can any of us do it? Maybe not, but if we are unhappy, perhaps we can improve our emotional state just enough for us to feel as though we are coping with life.

What Matters to You?

Perhaps it's this group of ideas:

- Status
- Wealth
- Success
- Confidence

How about these:

- Love
- Compassion
- Goodness
- Understanding

Or maybe it's these ideas:

- Education
- Friends
- Good looks
- Brains

A clever psychologist once told me that the first two groups look worthwhile but the one that's *really* worth pursuing is the third. Without a degree in psychology, all I can go on is a lifetime of experience, so it strikes me that at various times we need to aspire to every one of the things listed and a few others besides. So, if you are unhappy with yourself or your life, try this mindfulness meditation:

Just Breathe

- Don't try to achieve anything for the time being—just sit quietly and rest your hands on your legs with the palms down.

- Close your eyes.

- Focus on your breathing, but breathe normally rather than in an unusual or special way.

- If you find it hard to keep clutter or chatter out of your mind, imagine that you have a broom in your hand and that you are sweeping unwanted thoughts out of the way.

- Let your mind rest for a while.

- If that is all you need to do today, gently open your eyes.

- Consider how you felt during the meditation and see if you feel any different now.

Now come back to the world. If you do this exercise a few more times over the next couple weeks, you will definitely feel better, and you will be ready to embrace the future and all the nicer aspects of life.

Let It Go

If an emotion began to surface during the meditation, and if it is a nice one, embrace it and be happy. If it is a negative one, such as envy, anger, or guilt, remember this isn't part of you—it is just a phase—and that this is the time to let it go. Don't judge or criticize yourself. Forgive yourself. Think about those who have hurt you and know that their bad behavior is a measure of their small-mindedness, weakness, and selfishness, and be glad that you aren't like them. Admit to yourself that you are better than they are.

The Five Reiki Principles, Discovered and Taught by Mikao Usui

The following mantra is very well known, because it is the poem that Reiki practitioners learn. I can't say for sure that Mikao Usui wrote it, but it is attributed to him.

Just for today, do not be angry.
Just for today, do not worry.
Just for today, be grateful.
Just for today, work hard.
Just for today, be kind to others.

If one of the lines of the poem is bothering you today, try the following twist on the mindfulness meditation.

A Mindfulness Meditation

- Don't try to achieve anything for the time being—just sit quietly and rest your hands on your legs with the palms down.

- Close your eyes.

- Focus on your breathing, but breathe normally rather than in an unusual or special way.

- If you find it hard to keep clutter or chatter out of your mind, imagine that you have a broom in your hand and that you are sweeping unwanted thoughts out of the way.

- Let your mind rest for a while.

- Consider one of the lines of the Reiki poem that is bothering you today.

- See how you feel about it.

- Let anger or worry wash through you and pass on out into the universe without harming you or anyone else.

- If it is something worth doing, such as giving a day's work for a day's pay or being kind to others, consider how you would feel if you did that today to the best of your ability.

- Feel good about yourself and don't judge or punish yourself.

- Know you can be or do anything that you want—if you try.

- Gently open your eyes.

- Consider how you felt during the meditation and see if you feel any different now.

❄ ❄ ❄

15

A MEDLEY OF MEDITATIONS

Believe in yourself! Have faith in your abilities! Without a humble but reasonable confidence in your own powers, you cannot be successful or happy.

—Norman Vincent Peale

Meditating with Candles

Why do most people light a candle when meditating? Obviously, it creates the right ambience to bring you relaxation and calm, but more importantly, it gives you something to focus on. While looking at the flame of the candle, you are clearing your mind, and by concentrating on the flame, you are not allowing other thoughts that would distract from your meditation to enter your mind. This, in turn, will help you to make a faster connection with your higher self. I'm sure most of you have experienced the hypnotic effect that the flames from an open fire appear to have when you look at them. Candle meditation is a brilliant introduction if you have never tried it before, as concentrating on the candle flame will put you in the right space to go into your focused meditation.

If you want to focus your meditation on a specific subject, then it helps to use colored candles. Each individual color has its own meaning and will help you to meditate with more focus.

	White purity, peace, and truth. This color can be used in place of any other colors.
	Purple connects you to your higher self and psychic awareness.
	Blue opens the lines of communication for inspiration, happiness, and forgiveness.
	Green luck, money, success
	Pink love, harmony, friendships
	Yellow mental clarity, clairvoyance, confidence
	Red sexuality, passion, courage
	Brown getting your feet back on the ground
	Orange a good color for dealing with legal matters
	Silver psychic development, and it releases negativity
	Gold connecting with the spirit world
	Black destroys any negative energies around you and gives protection. This is an ideal color if you want to go into a deep meditation, for example, when wanting to investigate your past life.

These colors will become more familiar to you the more you use them. You will also note the connection to the chakra colors. Using a specific colored candle will help you achieve a more focused meditation or visualization. For example, meditating on a red candle will enhance your automatic writing.

The following list shows you how to use candles safely. This is especially important if you want to meditate with lit candles around, because being in a meditative state will make you less alert than you normally should be when dealing with fire.

• You must always ensure that you place your candle safely and that it is secure in the container. Do not place it on a surface that can burn. Do not place it anywhere near anything flammable. You need to ensure your safety before all else so that you can meditate without any concerns.

• Only use fresh candles. Light them only with a match, and snuff them out when you are finished. Do not blow them out. Always protect yourself before conducting any meditation with candles, as they are a very powerful tool.

• Make a mental note of how the candle flame burns.

• If you are aware of a good, strong flame, then you are ideally placed to begin your meditation. It also indicates that your meditation will work quickly.

• If, however, the flame is weak and small, you need to concentrate more and really focus on your meditation. It can also indicate that you are facing opposition, so this is what you need to prioritize in your meditation.

• If the candle starts to pop or make other noises, this is an indication that someone from the spirit world is attempting to communicate with you.

• If you should see a double flame while concentrating, then it indicates that you are not alone and someone is working either with you or against you. Your focused meditation can either enhance or dispel this.

• A flickering flame shows you that the spirit world is with you and is listening and that the spirits will be working on your behalf.

• If the candle burns down on only one side and there is no breeze in the room, it means that you have not concentrated enough on your meditation and that you need to do it again.

- If you see black smoke coming from the flame, then it is telling you that you are successfully ridding yourself of any negativity.

- If the flame is sparking, then you are not being realistic in what you are asking for.

Dreams

Sigmund Freud is quoted as suggesting that dreams are the window to our unconscious minds. If you think about it, when you are asleep you are in a deep meditative state, so it makes sense that you can experience anything while dreaming. It is also the ideal time for your spirit guides to communicate with you. Most of us know the saying "I'll sleep on it" and that really can help, because you may fall asleep with a particular problem on your mind and wake up with the solution. How many  times has this happened to you? I always tell people that they should listen to their dreams.

It is well documented that people experience premonition dreams. I had a very strange dream that is still vivid to me, which I now know was about the Twin Towers disaster in America on 9/11. My interpretation, however, was not of the Towers but of a huge, tall chimney that was attached to a factory-like building inside of which there were many people working. I saw the chimney collapse. I didn't even realize that this dream related to the Twin Towers until I was relaying my dream to a friend two weeks later. This was obviously the spirit world forewarning me of the impending disaster. It was interesting to discover that many of my psychic friends also received this message through varying dreams, including Sasha, who dreamed the night before the event of airplanes flying toward tall buildings and docking inside them like something

MY OWN DREAMS

Dreams not only enable the spirit world to communicate, but sleeping in a meditative state provides a pathway for your loved ones to visit you. Not long after my mother passed, she visited me in what I first thought was a dream, but it felt real and it woke me up. My mother was in my bedroom, sitting in a chair; she looked unbelievably happy and was beaming from ear to ear. She always had a beautiful smile, but this was something even more beautiful. She was talking to me but nothing was coming that I could hear. She turned away from me and looked behind her as if someone was standing at the back of her chair. She smiled again, looked back at me, and then just faded away into nothingness. I instinctively knew she had come to see me to give me assurance that she was fine, that she had passed into the spirit world without difficulty, and that she was being looked after.

You may think that I had purposefully dreamt this or that my mother had been on my mind prior to sleeping, but I can assure you that this was not the case as I had more important things on my mind at the time. Her appearance to me also told me that she is never far away from me. The fact that she had appeared in that way gave me peace of mind that enabled me to deal with the problems I faced at that time. Now, when I meditate, I always talk my problems over with my mother and ask for her help and guidance, particularly with any family problems.

Never underestimate your dreams!

from *Star Wars.* When we are in a deep meditative state, e.g., asleep, it is easier for our guides to communicate with us.

Why do you have recurring dreams and nightmares? Usually, it is something buried within the subconscious that is causing you to be anxious. When you experience this type of dream, interrupt it by asking your guides to show you what you should do. Ask for guidance and a solution. You may think you cannot do this while you dream about being chased or seeing something horrible, but if you meditate before you sleep, you can remain in control of your dreams.

If you need to find out the exact interpretation of any of your dreams, there is plenty of information available in books or on the Internet. You will find there is always a message contained within them, usually from your guides, no matter how random the dream appears to be. Once you have interpreted the dream, the message will become crystal clear.

A Christian Contemplation

Christians use the term *contemplation* rather than the word *meditation*. As you will see, however, the method is much the same as the kind of meditation in which one chooses a specific word as a mantra and focuses on it.

• Find a quiet place to sit and close your eyes.

• Choose a sacred word and focus on it.

• When thoughts intervene, come back to your sacred word.

• After about ten minutes, come back to the world, keeping your eyes closed for a few moments.

A Buddhist Meditation

You can start with an opening meditation or a yoga breathing meditation and then move on to this deeply philosophical meditation.

• May all sentient beings have equanimity, free from attachment, aggression, and prejudice.

• May they be happy and have causes for happiness.

• May they be free from suffering and causes for suffering.

• May they never be separated from happiness that is free from suffering.

Living in the Present

Rest your hands on your legs with the palms down and take regular breaths.
Focus on your breathing.

- When your mind wanders to the past, gently tap your left leg.

- When your mind wanders off to the future, gently tap your right leg.

- Whenever a thought arises, send it to the memory bin and refocus on
  your breathing.

Cosmic Ordering

There is a theory that you can ask
the cosmos to give you the things you
want—not to mention the things you
need! I am skeptical of this idea, because
if it worked, everyone's wishes would
be fulfilled, and while that may be the
case when we reach the spirit world, it
certainly isn't the case down here on
earth. However, a bit of cosmic ordering
might bring results, particularly if your
request isn't purely selfish.

Let us say you would like a pet for
yourself and your children. It's a nice idea, and this is how you might speed up
the process of finding just the right one.

- Do any kind of preparation or grounding meditation.

- Sit quietly and let your eyes close.

- Imagine the kind of pet you would like. See it as being the right size,
  color, type, and so on.

- Keep imagining the pet while it is playing, resting, eating, and being
  in the home surroundings.

- Imagine your children and the pet enjoying each other.

- Ask mentally for the right pet to find its way to you and for you to be able to give the pet a good life.

- Come slowly back to normality and open your eyes.

You can use the same technique for a better home for your family, a bit of land, getting a job or finding a better job, more money, a car for yourself or your children, or a million other things. Ensure your request isn't selfish and give it a go. The universe may give you what you *need* rather than what you fancy, but it's worth a try.

Astral Travel

Astral travel, or astral projection as it is now more commonly known, is something that can take months and months of practice. As with all meditations, it is necessary to have an open mind and to practice on a regular basis. Placing protection around yourself is absolutely essential!

What is astral travel? It is when your consciousness separates itself from the physical body and travels freely—also known as an out-of-body experience. I'm sure some of you may have felt the "bumpy landing" when you return from your journey back into your body, and you wake up from your sleep with a jolt—or you get that falling feeling. Some people will find astral travel easy to do while others will never experience it. It can be a frightening experience, but you never need to worry, as you will always remain attached to your body, no matter how far you travel.

Astral travel has been well recorded on numerous occasions by people who were seriously ill in hospital and who were under anesthetic during an operation. They have spoken of floating above the bed, watching the surgeons and nurses attending to them, and, after their experience, even being able to relay exactly what was happening and the conversations that were taking place at the time. You often hear of people traveling through a tunnel toward a white light, but being sent back as it is not their time to pass over. These examples are all a form of astral travel.

Deep meditation will help you achieve an out-of-body experience. However, this is not always the case. I had my very first experience when I was fourteen. I was walking down the main street behind my parents when I was suddenly floating above all of us, and I was watching myself walking across the road. I was not aware of a body—only that I was floating—but still attached to my body. It was like an invisible cord, but one that only I could see. It was as if my mind was in a balloon. I had no idea what was happening to me, and I confess that I found it very frightening. When I got home, I plunged my face into a basin of cold water. It was years later that I realized how privileged I was to have experienced this.

I have friends who regularly travel around the world. They are able to recall, with great precision, everything they have seen. Apparently, in the 1970s, the CIA showed extreme interest in astral travel, although they referred to it as "astral projection" or "remote viewing." Some of the experiments they conducted were very successful . . . others were not. However, it does somewhat prove that if you can master astral travel through deep meditation, you could have some wonderful experiences. There is no limit as to how far you can travel—even out into space!

CONCLUSION

By learning and practicing meditation, you will find that it can enhance your life. By conducting regular meditation sessions, you will discover that it opens up so much to you. It can improve your health, can give you solutions to problems, and may connect you to your higher self as well as to your spirit guides, angels, and the spirit world in general.

The key word is *practice*.

Meditation combined with visualization is extremely powerful, so be prepared for an exciting and interesting new time, particularly if you want to connect to the spirit world, as you will be opening the lines of communication through meditating and it will increase your psychic abilities. Meditation is also a great way of healing so many of life's problems.

There are now many ways you can join others in meditation, if you do not want to do it alone. You can join a spiritualist church, where members connect to the spirit world. Yoga groups also practice meditation as well as provide healthy exercises. In fact, there are many groups or clubs that you can join if you take the time to look for them. I prefer to meditate alone, so I do not get distracted, but it is obviously an individual choice.

This book, written with the assistance of friends and colleagues, attempts to give you many examples and different ways of meditation that we have successfully experienced ourselves, so we know they work.

I wish you all a very happy journey through your meditation!

❉　❉　❉

ACKNOWLEDGMENTS

Some of the meditations in this book have been kindly shared with me by a number of people over a long period. I would like to thank the following people accordingly:

- Eve Bingham

- The late David Bingham

- Jan Budkowski

- Barbara Ellen

- Sasha Fenton

- Joylina Goodings

- The late Gordon Arthur Smith

- Sonya Sharma

ABOUT THE AUTHOR

When Jackie was fourteen, she started to experience a range of psychic phenomena, some of which frightened her. Soon they stopped, though, and in time, she forgot about them. As life went on, Jackie went through the kinds of trials and tribulations that made her look for answers to the big questions, and this led her to an interest in spirituality.

Sometime later, she met the highly respected healer and medium Gordon Arthur Smith, who became a fond grandfather figure and a wonderful mentor. In time, this led to her becoming a medium, healer, Reiki master, qualified counselor, and tarot reader.

Jackie has served as secretary and later as president of the British Astrological and Psychic Society.

IMAGE CREDITS

INDEX